PR

Divine Aphasia

In a remarkable blend of literary creativity and clear accounting of her personal history, Nelson courageously recounts the profound joys and pains, the consequences good and bad, of growing up in an alcoholic family. Her own vigilance in pursuit of wholeness is evidenced by this intricately complex, brutally honest journey from eros to agape, including the formative experiences that lurk beneath those travels. An important, inspiring read for those who have been critical of themselves to the neglect of the impact of their impressionable years.

Jeanie O'Connor, D. Min, BCC, Director of Spiritual Care, Ascension Brighton Center for Recovery

Nancy Owen Nelson's *Divine Aphasia* is a courageous and compelling narrative that traces her lifelong journey in search of the lost father, which becomes, ultimately, a search for the self. It is a narrative that only builds in power, and along the way sustains moments of profound insight. We only grow through our struggles and this narrator examines her struggles unsparingly. The little girl who for most of her life ran after her father, crying, Daddy, wait for me! finally realizes: "I can stop looking for Dad. He's been here all the time." She gave a part of herself to each person she lost. The book asks: how can she gather all the pieces she gave along the way? She looks back at her other selves as a way forward, ultimately to a reconciliation with the father, and a deeper peace. This father, a flawed, giant of a man, is also the man who, on her 8th birthday, arranged for jets to skywrite her name across an "aqua blue sky." This man of few words carried with him the only word that mattered— her name.

Ann Putnam Ph.D., author of Full Moon at Noontide: A Daughter's Last Goodbye (University of Iowa Press)

Military life captured Lt. Colonel Woodford Owen Nelson, and its pressure spiraled him downward into alcohol abuse, which diluted his ability to show affection to his youngest daughter, Nancy Owen Nelson. The author experienced her father's painful Army career that included a major demotion and life-and-death decisions during the Cold War era. Military life, as shown in this memoir, may not be only a life dedicated to the service of country, but it can also be a journey into the dark and raw places that can damage souls. Her memoir is about finding answers. Nancy Owen Nelson shows her resilience and strength in investigating those shadows from her father's life and more. *Divine Aphasia* will assist readers to build an understanding of military life and the fathers who cannot fully create a loving place called home for themselves or their children. As a former military wife, and a college psychology professor, I recommend this memoir. It provides an avenue to understand how a childhood with a conflicted father can cast patterns of trauma-based decisions into that child's adult relationships.

Vicky Young, Ph.D., Faculty, Undergraduate and Graduate Programs; Human Development, Psychology, and Counselor Education, Prescott College, Arizona

Divine Aphasia

A Woman's Search for Her Father

Nancy Owen Nelson

The Ardent Writer Press
Brownsboro, Alabama

Visit Nancy Owen Nelson's Author Page
at

www.ArdentWriterPress.com

For general information about publishing with The Ardent Writer
Press contact *steve@ardentwriterpress.com* or forward mail to:
The Ardent Writer Press, Box 25, Brownsboro, Alabama 35741.

Cover art and composition are the work of Joel Geffen Photography and Cathy Dutertre using Photoshop techniques. The image on the front cover is supplied by Nancy Owen Nelson. Interior photos are supplied by Nancy Owen Nelson. Composition and cover are covered by the same grant for noncommercial use noted above.

Permission to use excerpts from *Waiting for Godot* is given by Grove Atlantic per Agreement #: PR-27158-30341, dated July 2, 2020 to the author, Nancy Owen Nelson.

Library of Congress Cataloging-in-Publication Data

Divine Aphasia: A Woman's Search for Her Father by Nancy Owen Nelson

p. cm.-(Ardent Writer Press-2019) ISBN 978-1-64066-096-0 (pbk.); 978-1-64066-107-3 (hdk); 978-1-64066-097-7 (eBook mobi)

Library of Congress Control Number 2020951542

Library of Congress Subject Headings
- BIOGRAPHY & AUTOBIOGRAPHY / Personal Memoirs.
- BIOGRAPHY & AUTOBIOGRAPHY / Women
- Autobiography--Personal narratives
- Autobiography--Miscellanea.

BISAC Subject Headings
- BIO026000   BIOGRAPHY & AUTOBIOGRAPHY / Personal Memoirs
- BIO022000   BIOGRAPHY & AUTOBIOGRAPHY / Women

Contents

ACKNOWLEDGEMENTS

THIS BOOK HAS BEEN a long time in the making. It's been through numerous drafts and working titles, it's been shared with trusted readers—Rick Bailey, Olga Klekner, Christy Rishoi, Larry Juchartz, and Vicky Young—who have provided feedback and support. Thanks to Joel Geffen for his hours of soulful conversation with me to create the cover. Thanks to my union president for his continued friendship and support. I thank Mary Edwards Wertsch, whose book, *Military Brats: Legacies of Childhood Inside the Fortress*, affirmed the unique challenges of life as a "brat."

Appreciation goes to Grove-Atlantic Publishing Company for permission to use brief passages from Beckett's *Waiting for Godot*, a play which, for most of my adult life, has echoed my search for meaning and has brought me comfort in knowing that I am not alone in my quest.

A version of the chapter, "Carpe Diem" was published in the online journal, *Reconceiving Loss*, in October 2013. The chapter, "Epiphany," was published in *The Wayne State Review*, 2016. The poems "Walking the Line with Johnny Cash" and "Steaming Concrete" were published in *Portals: A Memoir in Verse* (Kelsay, 2019).

To my agent, Kate Robinson, I give thanks for her friendship, her expertise in editing and publishing, and her guidance on the road to publishing this memoir. To Publisher Steve Gierhart, who gives his heart to his work, I extend appreciation for his care in bringing this book to life.

To my kin: your memories of my father may vary greatly from what you see here. They are, nonetheless, your memories. You loved him too.

Finally, I send deep thanks and love to my father, Lt. Col. Woodford Owen Nelson. Over fifty years after your passing, you are still with me. The journey of this book has brought you closer to me. And Dad, now I understand.

> Addendum: *Most names are changed. To readers who may recognize themselves or others in this book, I intend no harm to anyone. Please take me at my word, as I say in the Preface: "Now I know that these marriages were a pilgrimage to find, to fully understand my father, ... [and] why I married so many times."*

Divine Aphasia

To My Father
Woodford Owen Nelson

Song for a Winter's Night
after Gordon Lightfoot
after Joy Gaines-Friedler's "Burial"

I walk briskly in a neighborhood—it's silent,
still, green with lush trees, sheltered from
virus' evil grip. I listen to Lightfoot's ballad,
voice from my past, days when, an animal
caught in a trap of her own doing, I longed for
a tall, lean man with hands, long fingers,
whose arms circled around me and around me
until I was more arm, more hand, than body.

There were many winter's nights of longing for
that voice, raspy with smoke, yeasty smell of beer,
a voice that stoked fire in my belly with the hands
I loved as he fingered Petoskey stones, moved
them in those hands, those fingers, and between
puffs of smoke, rubbed them hard with coarse
sandpaper, then with soft polishing cloths.

Finally, rough stones would surrender to his touch,
relinquish roughness to polish, to long, stroking
fingers, to the glow of coral, a colony of tiny animals
trapped inside for billions of years.

But I did not stay the course. I left when yeasty
scent turned to rotten fruit, smoke filled my lungs,
my chest. When those fingers, those hands, held
only rough stones, ancient and unchanged.

I left before I was buried forever.

PREFACE

I HAVE BEEN MARRIED five times, the last one twenty years and counting. Two of my former husbands committed suicide. Now I know that these marriages were a pilgrimage to find, to fully understand my father, who died at the age of sixty-two. His problems with depression and addictions led to his early death. When Ted, my fourth husband, committed suicide two years after our divorce, I sought to understand why I married so many times and why I married Ted under challenging circumstances.

Ultimately, I realized I could only save myself.

"*Given the existence...of a personal God...with white beard...who from the heights of divine apathia divine athambia divine aphasia loves us dearly with some exception for reasons unknown but time will tell and suffers like the divine Miranda with those who for reasons unknown but time will tell are plunged in torment plunged in fire ...*"

— **Samuel Beckett** - Lucky, ***Waiting for Godot***

Moment of Clarity

1

A FAMILIAR FEELING envelops me as my husband Ted enters our house, red lipstick smeared on his mouth, the sense of unease that followed me into adulthood from my earliest childhood memory.

It has been one of those dark, frozen midwinter days in Michigan when the temperatures range from 0—10 F, the type of day that slips easily into long, heavy nights. On Wednesday night, our "night out" separately, my husband Ted always drinks at his favorite bar, and I see a movie or meet a friend for dinner. I arrive home before him and light the fire he's laid out for me earlier in the day. He lurches through the front door, but before he can close it, snow spits into the warm room. His grey knit cap and black coat are covered with ice crystals. He shakes them off and hangs the jacket and cap on the back of a chair to dry, moving from the shadows to warm himself before the fireplace, his long fingers fanning apart. He leans toward the flames, loses balance, and catches himself.

Even from my seat on the couch facing the fireplace, I smell beer and nicotine. Ted turns his face toward me to reveal the wide, uneven smear of red lipstick around his mouth. He is a clown with smudged makeup.

Did the topless dancers kiss him during his weekly excursion to a bar? I realize the dancing ladies have made Ted the butt of a joke. One of his "friends," probably Sherry, his favorite, has plotted to get him in trouble with me. I envision her and the others standing

1

around him as he perches on a bar stool, a half-empty beer mug sweating in his hand. He's been on that stool for several hours, drinking beer after beer and gazing steadily at the dancers, his glazed eyes mirroring them. Their breasts jiggle and bounce as one of them, then the next one, kisses him, leaving behind a fresh coat of lipstick applied just moments before. Fresh lipstick smudges best.

I'm surprised that even these women would make fun of a disabled man.

"You have lipstick all over your mouth." I speak slowly, enunciating my words. I point toward my face, as if I'm talking to a small child.

He laughs. Then he shuffles into the bathroom to look in the mirror.

While scrubbing his face with hand soap and rinsing with warm water, he hesitates. Then he speaks through the bubbles, water dripping off his chin. "They framed me. They played a trick on me." He's clear enough for me to understand him.

I say "good night" and nothing else. I turn toward the fire. As much as my chest and stomach clench in knots, I'm determined not to show my feelings.

I MARRIED TED, my fourth husband, in 1988, one and a half years after he suffered a stroke to his left brain.

Aphasia left his speech garbled and robbed him of the ability to understand anything said to him, a terrible irony when he had spent his professional life as a college English teacher. Throughout our five years of marriage, my son Owen and I, along with friends and family, communicated with him mostly by writing notes and, as time passed, by speaking very slowly. He tried to read our lips, and sometimes he could. But we always kept pen and paper nearby, just in case.

As I write this more than a decade after his death, I question myself as I have many times before. Why did I marry a man who was sixteen years older than I, who had suffered a stroke, and whose excessive smoking and drinking could not be ignored? During the months of our affair before his illness, I craved him. His skin—the scent of beer and the nicotine—seemed just like Dad's. After the stroke, it was a matter of honor. I had to be loyal, I told myself. I had to soldier on. I loved him, and as everyone around us believed, I had broken up his family. I feared he would return to his former wife, Darlene. I couldn't have that, could I? Suffer the embarrassment of having to give up my relationship and be alone again?

I know now that if I had left him then, few would have blamed me.

But I couldn't throw off that old mantra. *I love him. Maybe I can help him.*

The morning after Ted came home painted with lipstick, I wrote him a note:

> *What you do is your business. But I don't want to get gonorrhea, syphilis, or AIDS. Please let me know if you have sex with any of your lady friends.*

I wanted to make absolutely sure he understood me. I wanted him to know that I was standing strong, but separate from him.

I *really* wanted to shout, "It's over!" I heard myself say the words "I'm done." But I just couldn't say them yet. I was waiting for something, I didn't know what, to help me leave.

The same old feeling, wanting to leave. The feeling that made my stomach quiver with fear, the one that made me want to hide, to run away.

I wouldn't admit that the thought of leaving excited me. Although change is scary, I'd always looked forward to a rosy future, a time of possibility. To change and movement. Like the Army.

I'M THREE YEARS OLD, and I live with my parents and two older sisters in West Lafayette, Indiana. My daddy works at the university, teaching ROTC classes. One afternoon I'm sitting on the

3

hardwood living room floor, playing with my dolls and my favorite stuffed bear, Fido. The doorbell rings. Mom opens the door and there are men from the ROTC program in the doorway. Daddy hangs like a limp sack between two of them and one stands behind to hold him up. They don't say anything. The men undress Daddy down to his white boxers and t-shirt and carry him upstairs to my parents' bedroom. If there is any sound, it is of the men groaning and scuffling up the stairs carrying my heavy father. I watch his body slump and dip at the waist and he looks like the hammock hanging between two trees. Like the hammocks my teenage sisters Margie and Betty sleep on in the back yard some afternoons.

Margie isn't home this afternoon, so Betty takes me upstairs to my room and reads *The Three Little Pigs* to me. Something special must be happening because Betty just reads the story. She doesn't talk to me much, just reads the story. The late afternoon sun streams through the open window behind her. A breeze moves the curtains gently, like I'm supposed to feel calm but I don't. Betty tries to read the story like my teacher does, but she sounds scared, maybe angry. I wonder if she is mad at me.

"Take care the wolf does not catch you!" she recites. I can hear my sister's breath coming faster. Is Betty afraid too, like the pigs? I'm scared, but I don't really know why.

As the story goes on, the first two pigs aren't smart enough. They build houses that the wolf can blow down. Betty reads on, and her voice sounds like wood, hard and rough.

The third pig is smart, and he builds a brick house so the wolf can't blow it down!

"Now the wolf won't catch me and eat you!" Betty sounds out of breath.

This pig is safe!

As I listen, I pull my knees tighter into my body. My house could be blown down by a scary breath from the big, bad wolf! How can I be like the smart pig, safe in a house that won't disappear?

As Betty reads, a groan comes from the room across the hall. I hear a bedroom door close. The men clomp downstairs. I hear murmuring ... "Good afternoon, Mrs. Nelson," and then it gets really quiet. Always quiet after these things happen at my house.

The rest of the day, nobody talks about what happened. We pretend there is nothing wrong. Mom cooks dinner. We eat and then we listen to the radio show "Corliss Archer." We play some 78 rpm records on the old oak record player, Spike Jones' silly records with the musicians making farts or burp sounds. It reminds me of the night we went to a live concert with Spike Jones. How could Daddy fall asleep with all that noise?

Daddy stays upstairs in bed.

Why won't anybody talk about Daddy? Something must be wrong. It scares me when this happens, but every time he comes home acting funny, Mom and my sisters just get very quiet and act sad or mad. I can't tell which.

The next morning, after Daddy has gone to school, things go along as if nothing happened. Like I always do after Daddy comes home acting funny, I ask for a tea party with my stuffed animals on my parents' big bed. I sit in the middle of the bed, under the covers with big pillows behind me, and I put my animals—bears, rabbits, and puppies—next to me on both sides. Fido is closest to me because he's an old friend. He's a little brown bear, kind of raggedy looking. But I don't care. He's here with me and I'm happy.

Mommy brings me ladyfinger cookies and a cup of tea for a tea party in bed. Margie says that these cookies were made for kings, queens, and princesses. And today I'm a princess.

I know this is a special time, when Daddy has acted up again. I snuggle down under the faded pink bedspread, careful not to spill my tea and cookies. Yes, I am perfectly safe. The house won't fall down and I won't have to run and hide. That was yesterday. Today is happy.

Somewhere inside me, I know Daddy will act strangely again. I'd really rather not be a princess if it's because of Daddy.

Looking for Dad

2

Letter from Sister Betty
December 30, 1982

… We missed Dad so much during the war. All we thought of was "When Dad comes home we start to live again." Only it wasn't that simple. We left Ala., our roots were gone, and Dad was drinking. I always found a 'family' wherever I was—and in my eyes they had it made— all together and close. But when you looked closely they had their problems, too. I do think a lot of it, tho' was losing our roots. Seems people can plod along. Nothing ever changing, and have what we missed—or have the adventure we had without the security of old familiar things.

… Another factor I believe is … Mom and Dad were gypsies—but their parents were always there—giving stability. We're one generation away from that.

UNTIL I WAS FOURTEEN, my father, Woodford Owen Nelson (he went by "Owen") served in the U.S. Army. The nomadic lifestyle of a military family stayed with me years later, along with a sense that something wrong lurked behind every door I entered, every place we moved. We never stayed in any place for more than two or three years. But the constant moving wasn't the entire story. Dad's drinking took him away from us, even when he was present in the flesh.

Here, then gone.

When he was happy, he crowed a deep rousting laugh from his belly and wore a crooked smile. He charmed me into believing everything was just fine. At other times, he became a different person who rambled when he talked, who slurred his words.

A muffled silence, a whispering tension sat with our family at dinner or visited me in the night after I was supposed to be asleep. Perhaps because I was born thirteen years after my sister Marjorie ("Marge"), no one bothered to explain to me exactly what was happening. And in those days, no one talked about Dad's drinking.

Silence was the way to cope. Silence about the problem, silence broken only by the angry voice of my mother shouting down the basement steps to my father to be quiet as his laughter rose into the main floor and shattered her conversations with other wives over tea. On one of his binges, he'd taken to sleeping downstairs on an army cot with his bottle of whisky, a glass, and an ice bucket nearby. His constant oscillation between sober and drunk, and my oscillation between feeling happy and scared, were not unlike the movement of a military family—you leave old friends and you find new friends, you leave a school and a neighborhood to find another, you leave behind the familiar, and you face the new.

Because of these years, I came to believe that roots would tie me down, that I would disappear into mediocrity if I stayed in one place, around the same people. Now, more than five decades since my earliest recollections, I understand that this constant fluctuation became my way of understanding life. It's not about stability or home but about a desperate fear that I will somehow disappear if I stay too long in one place. This pattern infused itself into my consciousness like the cadence of a Sousa march playing over and over again, the needle stuck on a scratched 78 rpm record.

I THINK of my previous marriages, all four of them. They are like a slide show. As in the military life, I was always moving on.

I see myself, a young college student in the 1960s, with my first husband, Henry. I'm sitting on the bathroom floor in our student apartment, my ears stuffed with Kleenex, reading the poetry of Sir Thomas Wyatt, or perhaps William Wordsworth, for the next day's English class. Despite the Kleenex, I still hear the loud voices of Henry and his law student buddies discussing torts and the Miranda law. Henry sounds silly, the way he laughs so loud, like a hyena. His friends sound more dignified, but his voice seeps under the bathroom door and pierces through the Kleenex. I'm frustrated, kind of embarrassed for him.

With my second husband Bill, we discover soon that we are like oil and water. Not only do we not mix, but we don't understand one another. We feed each other's worse selves. We live with dissension, trying to make it work, for five years. Ten months after my son is born, I take my baby and leave Bill, and move to a city to take a college teaching job.

With my third husband, Evan, I spend evenings at fine restaurants and the symphony. He owns his own business and he works hard trying to be a father to my intelligent and hyperactive three-year-old son, Owen, whom I named after Dad. Evan is persistent. He endures the tantrums, even having his shins kicked by an angry little boy. After much effort on his part, Owen finally accepts him.

But I need excitement, someone who will be a challenge, have an edge.

After a year and a half of marriage, I leave Evan for Ted, my faculty colleague.

Marriage, for me, is like the Army, always another assignment, another new place, new friends, the excitement of change.

Don't stay too long in one place. If you do, you might disappear.

These must be my marching orders. Just like a soldier at war, I had to do what I was told. But these orders came from within me, not from outside.

Roots

3

I COME FROM A LINE of blessed folk who believed in the Holy Trinity and Jesus as the Son of God, straight from Southern Methodist Church doctrine. Woodford Owen Nelson was the first son born to Steve and Ellie Nelson, and they wanted him to serve God as a man of the cloth, a preacher.

Ellie and Steve Nelson ("Mama and Papa Steve"), along with "Big Mama" Chandler, my mother's stepmother, were home base for us. During all those years of driving the blue highways of our country, most every summer our family made it back to Hartselle, Alabama for a visit to the little Nelson house on Hickory Street. They were the closest thing to home.

Usually when we arrived, I was tired and sweaty from the long drive. I chose to run around the house from the side yard to the front porch. As I hurried up the steps, I could still hear the humming in my ears of tires against the concrete roads. There Mama Steve would be, smiling at me from her front door. She often wore a cotton housedress and granny shoes with high tops, much like the ones I would buy thirty years later to be in fashion. She'd hold the screen open with her thin arm and say, "Get in this house!" I knew I could look forward to good food and long conversations with cousins, aunts and uncles, on the front porch after dinner.

At her house, a meal as simple as lunch was legendary—sliced tomatoes from a local farmer's market, cold fried chicken and okra from the night before, tall glasses of iced tea with lemon and sugar, fresh biscuits, and some kind of cake or pie, home-baked. The aroma of the food filled the kitchen and met us as we entered the small side porch. From this entryway, Mama Steve usually stood to send us away when our visit was finished.

Papa Steve provided another kind of comfort. He had that gruff, loving quality of solid country folk. I remember how he rolled his own cigarettes with Bull Durham tobacco. I loved the little paper disks with the bull printed on them. He saved the disks for me for our visits, from one year to the next. I would come upon him in the living room, rolling a cigarette. In his later years, he would stare into the blank space created by his late-life blindness. Blind or not, he knew when I entered the room, could sense me if not see me. He could still tell a dime or a quarter from a nickel by touch, and, like many men of his generation, his main show of affection was with rough humor, as when he would rub his unshaven face against my tender cheeks.

One of my favorite photos shows Mama and Papa Steve on the front porch. Papa Steve stands to Mama Steve's left, his hand on her left arm, as if he is pulling or shaking it. Mama Steve, in her pale housedress, looks at Papa Steve with a girlish smile.

WHETHER MOM'S STATEMENT about Dad being the black sheep is true or not, I think that he believed it. I never actually witnessed Mama and Papa Steve's disappointment in their son's choice of career. But the feeling was just there, like the other elephants that filled the rooms of our many houses and apartments.

Maybe it was because Dad was so different from the rest of the family. While his siblings stayed close to home.... businessmen, Dad chose what his parents thought was an odd career—the military, with all ifs traveling…, especially drink. I imagine it was because he never became a preacher as his folks wanted, and because he chose what they thought an odd lifestyle of career—military, with all its traveling and the temptations of drink and gambling, especially drink. A few years back, I came across Mary Edwards Wertsch's book *Military Brats: Legacies of Children Inside the Fortress*. When I read her discussion of the "partnership" of alcohol and the military, the high level of tolerance for excessive use of alcohol by the uniformed, my mind opened to new understanding. Wertsch gave me a language and a sense that I'm not alone, but one of a "lost tribe," as author Pat Conroy labels military brats in the book's preface.

In the Bible belt country of serious churchgoers, alcohol was not tolerated in any form, though I was told that Papa Steve hid his "medicine" in the back of a closet or china cabinet.

Despite the fear of divine retribution, my father certainly experienced liquor in his younger years. He and his friends often drove to bootleggers in the neighboring German community of Cullman. But when Dad entered the urban Methodist Birmingham-Southern College in the fall of 1923, he found a world inhabited by the liberal use of alcohol. Even though the college banned booze on campus, he'd talk about how the frat boys managed to purchase and consume it. Owen was a college man, and he was away from home. No preacher's robe draped his shoulders.

DAD TOLD STORIES from his "growing up," about playing football in a pasture while sliding on cow manure to touchdowns, and about dating the daughter from the only Jewish family in town. In the 1920s, there were few Jews in the South. Some towns had only one family. So, Dad's dating the Jewish girl was notable, he thought.

Like many young men, Dad's early work life was spotty. As a boy, he worked in a local dry-cleaning store. Later he became a cotton buyer and then an investigator for the IRS. When at sixteen years old he lied about his age to enroll in the Alabama National Guard, he found his passion. He maintained this commitment from the late 1920s into the 1940s, when the possibility of U. S. involvement in war became imminent, and he enlisted in the Regular Army. He had found his path, his career.

In Owen Nelson's scrapbook, he had more photos of his men and muddy construction sites than he did photos of Betty, Marjorie, or Mom, (although he did name his jeep "The Betty and Margie"). I'm told his men loved being under his leadership. Before Truman integrated the Army in 1948, he wrote Mom from New Guinea and asked Mom to ship black-eyed peas and turnip greens. He made a southern meal for his black soldiers and he ate with them. Since he was an occasional Army chef, I imagine he made cornbread too.

One story goes that Dad's men in the National Guard unit, Company E Sheffield, went on active duty and were stationed in Alaska. He had recruited the men from his Sunday School class, and when he returned home on leave, he held a meeting at the church for the guys' families. He answered all of the mothers' questions about their sons, including who had lost or gained weight and how much.

"How did you remember all of those details?" Betty asked.

"I didn't," he answered. "I just wanted the mothers to feel good about their boys."

Dad's mothering tendency was apparent in his last appointment as Army Representative to the National Guard Unit in Sault Ste. Marie, Michigan. I remember his retirement party, when his men presented him with luggage, a Stetson hat, and a monogrammed military baton. And I remember tears in the eyes of several of them. The baton, with "Lt. Col. Woodford Owen Nelson," rests on a bookshelf in my study.

Many stories I've been told about my father emphasize his sense of kindness and justice to the ordinary people. His black-and-white World War II photos, faded and preserved on the crinkling pages of a scrapbook, show the black soldiers he mentored. During World War II, when my sister Betty's classmates were voicing hatred of the "Japs," he told her, "There's enough hate in the world. Don't add to it."

My father showed compassion for people in need. Near the end of his life, he paid for a poor girl's piano lessons anonymously. Betty told me that a girl in her class came to school underdressed in the middle of freezing winter. Betty told Dad about her, and the next day Dad came to school carrying a new, warm coat. I can envision the girl entering the classroom, shoes and clothing worn, a thin sweater over her shoulders. Her cheeks are red from the cold, and she rubs her hands together to warm them. My father gives the coat to the teacher. The girl is called out of the room and when she returns, she wears a brand-new coat. I can imagine her face open up with surprise, then disbelief, then a tentative smile.

While Dad never saw combat directly, he wasn't without the scars of war. He suffered an ulcer while in New Guinea. At one point in his service, he walked into a general's tent to find a man holding a knife to the general's throat. Dad shot and killed him. It was his duty. He never said much about it, so all I know is that it happened. I can only imagine how this incident must have haunted him.

He followed orders.

Protect the commander at all costs.

I WAS BORN IN 1946, on the cutting edge of the post-war baby boom generation. My two sisters welcomed me very differently.

Betty was sixteen at the time, and she was embarrassed at the evidence that her parents had "done it." I don't remember much about her, except that she stayed to herself. She was busy dating and trying to get away from home and Dad's drinking. She married in 1950, when I was four years old. She was in love with a soldier, Dwayne.

Marge, age thirteen, treated me as if I were her own child. She loved and nurtured me from my birth until she left the family to marry Rob when I was eleven. Marge was the one I remember most during this period. Mom and Dad, and Betty all fade into grey. Marge was my heroine. I adored her.

I recall Marge on afternoons after school, when she hurried from the school bus and into the house. Her lanky legs carried her athletic frame, and her long, brown wavy hair lifted off of her shoulders. I'm told that before she did anything else, she'd rush to my room. She stopped only to throw down her books and sweater. She picked me up, cradling me against her shoulder, her brown waves falling over my face. "How's my sweet Nancy?"

The family Christmas card in 1947 is a professional photograph of my sisters and me. I was one-and-a-half years old. Betty, on the left, is dressed in a formal suit coat and smiles only slightly, her face framed with her dark, shoulder-length curls. Marge is on the right, and her hair falls to the sides of a deep-dimpled smile. I gaze into the camera with a serious expression, my fine, almost non-existent hair brushed to the top of my head into a single curl. Dad signed the card "From the 3 girls."

That fall of 1947, Dad was appointed to teach ROTC at Purdue University, West Lafayette, Indiana. This is where I first remember my family.

West Lafayette, Indiana

4

BETWEEN THE FALL OF 1947 and the summer of 1951, we lived across the street from West Lafayette High School on Grant Street in a two-story house with a backyard. Our family life was centered on Dad's ROTC duties at Purdue University and Mom's social obligations as a military wife, serving tea to other military wives and attending the ladies' bridge club. Dad often brought male students home from his classes. These guys gave the two pretty girls in our house their full attention. There were military balls, and evenings when family and guests gathered around the piano while my mother played, and we sang.

ONE NIGHT, sometime when I'm quite small, my sisters are with friends in the living room. They are laughing loud. I'm on the floor, playing with my Lincoln Logs.

Daddy stumbles into the room with a bare chest. He's drawn bright red circles around his nipples with Mommy's red lipstick. He smiles his one-sided grin and laughs. "I have tits too!" he says.

My sisters' friends are quiet for a moment or two, and then everyone sounds like they're trying to laugh when they don't want to. What are tits? I guess he's not supposed to say that word.

I crawl into a corner and curl up. I want to hide.

That's not so bad as the night Mommy, Betty, and Marge go across the street at the high school football game and leave me with Daddy. We're upstairs in the bedroom. Soon he falls asleep in an easy chair by the bedroom window. He snores and snorts every few minutes, so loud I sometimes think the neighbors might hear.

I perch on a straight chair by the window, my chin on the paint-chipped sill and my forehead pressed against the screen. I see the stadium, the many people just across from our house. The crowd cheers when something exciting happens.

I've been so scared for such a long time.

After a while, I begin to call out through the screen—"Mommy, Mommy"—but no one can hear me, even Daddy, who's right next to me. I keep thinking I see my mother and sisters in the crowd, that when they hear me, they will come home. Daddy wakes up only a few minutes before I hear the front door open.

Why does Daddy sleep so much? Why doesn't he remember I'm here?

BECAUSE I WAS SO YOUNG in West Lafayette, one to four years old, what happened moves through my memory as a series of still shots. An image pauses, then moves forward for the next one.

I remember riding with Daddy in our brown coupe. He let me drive sometimes while I sat in his lap, my hands on the steering wheel along with his. With his arms encircling me, I knew I was safe, and I felt important.

Once we drove to a jewelry store, just us two. This trip was very special because we didn't usually do anything together. In the store, we looked at rings for little girls. Dad asked me which one I wanted, and I pointed to a gold ring with a little blue stone in the middle. The stone looked like a planet. He told me it was turquoise.

I would wear that ring for a long time, even after I became a grown woman, when it was the perfect pinky ring. Years later after

Dad was dead, I lost the stone and replaced it with another. I wanted to keep it like it was. I wanted that moment in the jewelry store to last, Dad's hand on my shoulder—Forever.

Other disconnected memories made me love our life in West Lafayette—our midwestern house on a street across from the high school, the Floyd twins, who lived down the street. The boys played with me and made me laugh by teasing me with the jingle, "Nancy has ants in her pants!" Even though they teased me, I knew they liked me.

I recall my first Halloween in West Lafayette. I was a ghost wearing a white sheet over my head with eyeholes cut so I could see. Margie walked with me. The street was dark except for the porch lights, and my shoes crunched in the dry leaves.

In summer, dandelions spread a yellow carpet in our front yard, and I picked them as if they were precious flowers. I didn't know they were weeds. They are beautiful to me, the yellow, tiny petals shooting out from the center, like the sun I drew in my pictures for Mom. Some summer afternoons Marge and Betty sunbathed in the back yard while I made crowns and bracelets with the stems of white clover.

But no one ever talked to me about Dad, about what was the matter with him.

AT FOUR YEARS OLD, I spent much time inside my imagination. Since these were the days before television, radio drama was a favorite entertainment for the family. I especially liked "Corliss Archer," a program about a cute high school girl with a boyfriend who lived next door to her. She had a regular family, with a father and mother, and her dad never drank or acted strange. She never seemed afraid and talked about school and friendships. I wanted to be Corliss. One day at play school, the teacher called the class roll and I answered "Corliss."

Mom took Corliss Archer home that afternoon.

TOCKIE WAS an imaginary girl everyone, even Dad, accepted into the house. She was my best friend. Mom would set a place for her at the table and I made her eat my carrots and peas when I didn't want them. She spent time with me, and then I didn't feel lonely. I called Tockie to me when I overheard my Daddy snoring; or when I could tell something was wrong, and everybody's faces got tight and they stopped talking.

My mom played piano almost every day. Melodies floated through our home at all times of the day. My sisters taught me "Row, row, row your boat, gently down the stream." But I sang it differently, the way I thought was right. "Merrily, merrily, merrily, merrily, life is *butter* dream." Many times, as I sat on the wooden floor near the piano and watched the little sunbeams float in the air, I was happy. I rocked back and forth, my legs straight out and my arms moving back and forth to row a boat. "Row, row, row your boat."

Sometimes the music made me sad. When my sisters brought boys to our house, we gathered in the living room. The boys wore uniforms like Dad's. Everyone stood around the piano while Mom played "Stardust," "St. Louis Blues," or "As Time Goes By." I balanced on tiptoe to watch my mother's spider-like fingers move fast over the keys. The light was dim because of our dark curtains, and I could barely see my pretty sisters. Betty sometimes wore spike heels, the kind she had on when she fell down the stairs from the second floor, and a dressy dress, and her long black hair plunged in curls onto her shoulders. Margie was taller. She wore Oxford saddle shoes, a plaid wool skirt and sweater, and her light brown hair covered part of her face as she leaned over the piano to sing. When she smiled, her dimples showed deep in her cheeks.

In this scene I'm remembering, Dad was not there, and no one said anything about him. But I could still feel him, as if he was in the room.

I was only four, but I already knew by heart the songs my mother played. I tried to sing along with everyone, but the notes stuck in my throat. My mother seemed sad too, even as she sat on the piano bench, back straight and proud. To break the mood, she sped up her spider fingers and gave us "Kitten on the Keys."

The songs that made me the saddest were "Good night Irene, I'll see you in my dreams" and "Sentimental Journey." That last song was about going to some new place. I never want to leave our two-story white house across the street from the high school.

Somehow, I knew we wouldn't be staying for long.

Looking back, I can't put a particular meaning to my sadness. I just know that I had a stitch in the throat when music poured from the piano, or when my mother sang. I had trouble singing the songs through. Maybe it was the words about love and beauty, or about home. Maybe it was the melodies, intoning something beautiful, something I could not reach or hold onto.

Into the Cold and Dark

5

DURING THE SUMMER OF 1951, our family lived in Decatur, Alabama while my father was deployed to Alaska. He would send for us when he was settled. We rented a house down the street from my step-grandmother, Big Mama Chandler. I had a boyfriend, Bobby, who lived a few houses from us. As far as I knew, he'd lived in the same house for his whole life, which was all of five years. During that whole summer, Bobby was always around. Sometimes in the hot afternoon, we walked to a gas station or grocery store to buy candy and ice cream. Afterwards we'd amble back to Big Mama's house with our ice cream cones or popsicles, kicking stones along the uneven, cracked sidewalk speckled with patches of sunlight amongst the shade. Huge elm trees with wide trunks invited my fantasies.

Because the afternoon was hot and humid, the ice cream dripped down our arms. Bobby and I didn't want to waste one drop of the delicious, sticky stuff, so we licked our arms from elbows to wrists, then our hands and fingers. Big Mama Chandler had a shady front porch, and we sat on the steps to finish our ice cream.

Down the hill beside the house was the tiny sloping sidewalk—to me, like a fairy path. Bobby and I walked on it to the creek behind the house.

Bobby skipped stones on the creek. I tried to do the same, but I wasn't able to make my stones skitter and skim on top of the water like his. Soon we would grow tired of the stones and the heat and climb back up the hill to the front yard to sit under an elm tree. We made up stories about The Roy Rogers and Dale Evans western show and dug up imaginary roads and horse trails around the tree's roots with sticks.

That summer, when we weren't together, Bobby and I would call each other on the phone and read books without speaking, the phone to our ears.

I didn't realize how different his body was from mine until one day I went to his house while his mother bathed him. She called me into the bathroom while she was soaping him. *He doesn't look like me down there*, I thought. He looked like he had a little Vienna Sausage between his legs.

This was about the time I began to have strange feelings in my stomach when I would stroke my teddy bear Fido. I liked the way it felt, but I told no one, and I couldn't explain what I was feeling.

Bobby helped me get through the months before we moved to Alaska. For that entire summer of 1951 while we played, I knew that my family would soon make a major change. We would desert the warm, sunny South for a strange, cold, and dark place, leaving behind everything we knew. My sister Marge would go with us, but Betty and her husband, Dwayne, would move to Bowling Green, Kentucky, where she would soon deliver her baby.

Still, the idea of Alaska was magical. I "played Alaska" to imagine what it would be like. One afternoon Bobby and I covered the entire living room, furniture and floor, with tissues. We thought it looked like snow. Mom was not happy when she found her living and dining room covered in white. Bobby and I had to clean up the "snow" and put it back in its box.

By mid-winter 1951, it was time to join Dad in Alaska, where he was a Battalion Commander at Ladd Air Force Base. I didn't want to leave Bobby. How could I find other friends like him in that cold place, up near the North Pole, where it was dark?

Mom, Marge and I boarded a train in Decatur, Alabama headed for San Francisco. There we would board a ship that would take us along the Pacific coast of Canada to Anchorage, Alaska. Our journey on the train lasted several days and nights, so we had sleeping cabins. I was excited about having the little bed where I could lie down and peek through the curtains and watch the lights, towns, and deserted streets pass until I fell asleep. I loved the fancy dining room with little pats of butter molded with the imprint of a cow. I wanted to save my butter patty until we arrived in Alaska, but Mom laughed and told me it would be in bad shape by that time.

Marge had the flu and spent most of the trip in her berth. She was so sick that the engineer radioed ahead for a doctor at one of the cities where we stopped. We expected Betty's baby, Mom and Dad's first grandchild, to be born during our trip, in Bowling Green, Kentucky. The train went through Bowling Green without stopping. All we could do was watch the town disappear.

The boat trip from San Francisco to Anchorage, Alaska took a week, and choppy seas made Marge sicker. One afternoon, the ship horn bleated like a hurt animal and the speaker ordered "All passengers on deck, with life jackets." It was only a drill, they said, but I was frightened by the horn, the rough sea, and the grey skies. I know now that I was frightened, too, about what might lie ahead of us—a new, strange place with new friends and a new school.

When I talk with my sister Betty recently about this trip, she recalls that Dad was with us. He met us in San Francisco. I have no memory of him until we arrived in Anchorage. The long train ride, and boat trip—to me, it was just us girls.

MY FIRST ALASKA MEMORY is of bouncing around in an Army airplane in the dark above snow-covered ground, from Anchorage to Fairbanks. Daddy is with us now, and the plane acts like a roller coaster. He's throwing up in a paper bag at the same time the pilot invites my sister Marge, who's feeling better, to the cockpit to watch them fly the plane. I think it's because she's pretty that Marge gets to go watch the pilots. I peer out of the frosted window at the snowy ground racing past us below. We land in the dark. The only lights I see are tiny, flickering, along the sides of the short runway.

The moment we depart from the plane, I feel the strangeness of Alaska. Tonight, the snow is deep. A man's voice, muffled through my thick earmuffs, speaks, "You'd better carry her high, Colonel. She'll get buried in all of this damned snow." As my dad lifts me up, all I can see is a clear sky with stars. I wish I could fly through that sky, up to the stars, just like we did in the airplane!

Someone else says it's 30 below. My nose and cheeks burn, and the night smells like a freezer when I open it to get ice cream.

The next morning, Mom climbs upstairs from our basement apartment to pick up some small cartons of milk that were delivered. She chops the milk into pieces so I can eat my Cheerios. My teeth hurt when I crunch the icy milk.

FOR ME, Alaska was about the extremes of light and darkness. The winters we spent there in 1951 and 1952 seemed endless. Depending on the month, the sun only rose for a few minutes, or for an hour or two. Had I been an adult, I might have thought of Sartre's *No Exit*, in which the characters come to realize that they are trapped for eternity with one another in a hotel that is Hell. As a young girl, all I knew was that I had to ride the school bus to the Little Red Schoolhouse for kindergarten. It was dark and the stars were out. On many morning rides to school, I leaned my head against the frosted window and watched the shimmering Northern Lights move across the sky. They reminded me of blinking Christmas lights.

The Little Red Schoolhouse was a warm, bright place to be during the day, but when I left to ride the bus home, the dark engulfed me again. It seemed to be waiting for me. I was always happy to see Mom waiting at the bus stop outside our brick apartment building, wrapped in her long coat with a fur hood and wearing brown mukluks, thick, warm snow boots made of seal skin and rabbit fur.

We were warned to protect ourselves from the severe cold, sometimes forty or fifty below zero. The newspapers and the base radio told us "Be sure to dress warm, in layers. Wear socks and gloves to avoid frost bite." Folks like us who lived on base walked through underground tunnels to shop, to visit friends, or to see movies. The darkness invaded the tunnels, which looped around endlessly like so many hoses tangled together. Some kids roller-skated in the tunnels, but I was afraid even to walk alone to my friends' apartments. I feared getting lost because the tunnels all looked alike; as I would round a curve, my heart would jolt if I heard echoes of a footstep or the whining of roller skates. I remember the tunnels were like low-lit metal tubes with few signs or directions. If I touched the walls, they were cold, like steel. Years later when I watched a Vincent Price movie, I had the same feeling of being in the dark, unpredictable tunnels.

One night, Dad and I walked through the tunnels to a game of poker. As usual, I was excited just to be with him, even if I didn't care about the game. The darkened poker room had a bar. The only light hung above the playing table. I remember the blues, reds, greens, blacks, and whites of poker chips and red pattern on the backs of the playing cards. Through the smoke, I watched a game I didn't understand. I drifted off to sleep on the hard, wooden seat of a booth nearby. It seemed like just a minute passed when Dad brought me a glass of ginger ale, bubbles rising from the bottom of the glass. There were no sounds other than the murmuring of the men at their game, no other scent but the cigarette smoke floating above the table.

I was there with my dad and I was safe with him. He would take care of me.

At five years old, I had no notion about the strategic importance of Alaska to our country's Cold War strategy. Ladd Air Force base was one of the northern-most surveillance sites, a "front line," so to speak, to identify and destroy any attackers headed south from the Soviet Union.

I now comprehend the importance of our location, but as a small child, the only clue I had was my dad's secretive exits during the night.

I'M TUCKED INTO BED, warm even though the chill of the Alaska night seeps in around the edges of our windows. I'm fast asleep when a loud siren blasts the quiet like a battle horn. I hear murmuring, somebody moving about our apartment, and then the door closes firmly. Daddy is gone again into the night. This is called an *alert*, and he has to go. Something might be happening with the Russians.

"When your dad is called away like this, he doesn't know where he is going, or when he'll come back. He might have to go somewhere secret and do an important job." Mom tells me this each time he leaves in the night. I lie in my warm bed wishing he had kissed me goodbye before he left.

During high alerts, especially when there is light, we're told not to look out our windows, but to stay away from them and close all of our curtains. Our apartment is in the basement, and one day, against the rules, I climb on a chair and peek out of our ground-level window. I can see the blades of grass in the lawn outside.

I feel small down here in the basement, with the grass at eye level. I watch soldiers in uniforms with helmets play hide and seek around some tall fir trees. They have long guns. It's fun to watch. But like the ship horn, like the siren in the night, these games give me knots in my stomach. Many nights I wake up to darkness and total silence. I wait for the siren, hoping Dad won't have to leave again.

SOMEHOW, the teachers make the Little Red Schoolhouse a happy place for us to learn. One day when it's starting to get darker and darker, my teacher helps us get ready for Parents' Day. We're supposed to make a copy of ourselves by lying down on a big piece of paper. A classmate draws an outline of us. I cut out my outline, and then I draw my face, my hair, fingers and nose, and color in my brown dress. I make my hair as curly as it really is, swirling a light

25

brown crayon around the edges of my face. I draw a smile, and then put the new "me" into my desk chair. I hope Mom will recognize me! I also put a drawing I had made of her on the bulletin board. In my picture she's wearing her brown dress, smiling big, standing on a green, grassy hill, not snow, and a huge sun hangs directly over her head. I write "The sun shines on Mommy" across the top of the picture.

The picture is the first thing she sees when she comes into our room. She smiles a big smile, just like the picture. And she's even wearing the brown dress! It must make her glad to see her picture, a happy mother after the darkness has gone away. A mother with the sun shining on her.

In kindergarten, I want to be the best student in the class. I want to impress my teachers. For Columbus Day, Mom and I write a song to play and sing for my class.

> Columbus sailed across the sea,
> to find this land for you and me.
> His cradle boat rocked low and high,
> and seemed to sing a "lullaby."

My teacher Mrs. Kiilsgaard loves my song!

SUCH REMEMBERED IMAGES of Alaska stay with me because this place was different from anything I had experienced in my short lifetime. The sunshine on the snow looked like crystals. Icicles hung long and sharp off the eaves of our apartment house. I would knock an icicle down with a snowball and suck it, cold and smooth on my tongue. Mom loved the winter too, walking with a general's wife over the frozen river. She wrote poems about the river and the trees, the snow coating everything like icing. "This is the most beautiful place we've ever lived," she exclaimed more than once.

My sister Marge, eighteen at the time, worked magic for me. Perhaps she understood that such a strange place as Alaska could be scary for a little girl. The Tooth Fairy visited often, but one time in particular, I had real proof of her existence. On awaking one morning, I found a shiny quarter on my pillow but tiny, brown footprints across my pillowcase.

I've often wondered how Marge was able to paint those tiny steps, what she used, and how she managed not to wake me.

Christmas was distinct because of our proximity to the North Pole, where Santa lived. This meant an early bedtime on Christmas Eve, but only after listening to "The Littlest Angel" on the radio.

TOMMY WAS A FRIEND I visited often. I had to walk through the tunnels to get to his apartment. I liked to play with him even though nobody could replace Bobby. Tommy made me feel less alone. When Tommy's family was transferred back to the lower forty-eight, their plane crashed, and the whole family died. I remember hearing the news in a room with indirect light, burnished and golden. I remember my mother talking about Tommy dying. I didn't understand, but somehow it felt like the dark again, like Daddy leaving—something in my stomach, eating it up.

What is it like to be dead?

WHILE DARKNESS DOMINATED half of the year, the coming of light in the spring and summer put a different cast on the Alaska experience. The sun set for only a few minutes, allowing the growth of giant-sized tomatoes and yellow squash. We attended unlit baseball games that lasted past midnight. The June 20, 1952 Ladd Air Force Base newspaper, *Midnight Sun*, called the following day the Summer Solstice, the "day the sun never goes out of sight—unless you are standing in a hole somewhere." That month, Ann Blyth, Gregory Peck, and Anthony Quinn came to Fairbanks to film *The World in His Arms*. Marge took a picture of Ann, and she was in the crowd scenes filmed on base.

OUTSIDE OUR APARTMENT building, on the big field where kids play in the summer, the Army battalions march in formation to a band playing a Sousa march. One afternoon I stand with my mom and sister, watching Dad's battalion go by us. He marches on the front corner, and he's very close to me. He stares straight ahead as if in a trance, growling orders that come from deep in his chest—"One, two, three, four." I'm standing so close to him, and I'm so proud. I yell—"Daddy, Daddy!" I want him to see me and wave, but he won't look at me. He just keeps marching and growling orders. His eyes look straight in front of him. I'm invisible.

I understand now why he didn't look at me as much as he wanted to. I imagine his face struggling to remain stiff, fighting against the crooked smile forming on his face, the right side of his mouth trying to lift in response to my calling out to him. He was such a soldier first. He had to control his face. He could not smile.

But back then, I didn't understand why he wouldn't look at me.

ONE PHOTO from Alaska best represents my experience there. Marge took it right after we had looked at a huge bear in the University of Alaska Museum. To me, the bear seemed twenty feet tall, but when as an adult, I see him in a 1954 *National Geographic Magazine* on Alaska. The bear is only nine feet tall. When I gazed up at him, I became invisible. Just minutes later, after we left the museum, I was alone in an empty field somewhere on the university campus. In the photo, I look so tiny that you can't really see my face at all, just a vague smudge on top of my body. If I am smiling, you can't tell.

No one else is around.

Desert of the Heart: Texas-Oklahoma

6

AFTER LEAVING ALASKA in early May 1953, our family was stationed at Wolters Air Force Base in Mineral Wells, Texas, where my father was again a battalion commander.

I would spend grades one, two, and part of three in Mineral Wells, Texas.

It was here that I really began to seek attention from others. I felt Dad pull further and further away from me. I needed affirmation.

As I remember it, Mineral Wells was hot most of the time. Even on Christmas Day, it was in the seventies. The dry Texas heat dehydrated me and left me nauseous and dizzy. The faucet water tasted like iron. Our brick school building looked as old as Mrs. Sears, my second grade teacher. In a black-and-white photo of me with the building as backdrop, I ride a pony and take my turn with the other kids.

One day in second grade, I entered my classroom carrying a bag with my ballet shoes and my pink ballet costume of lacy ruffles. I was taking ballet lessons at the time. I whispered to Mrs. Adams, asking if I could dance for the class.

"Can I?"

She corrected me.

"You should say 'may' instead of 'can,' Nancy. And yes, you *may*."

In the girls' bathroom, I changed into my pink tutu with a net skirt, tights, and ballet shoes. I returned to our classroom. "Nancy will dance for us today." Mrs. Adams smiled as she spoke. I climbed onto the top of her desk, careful not to fall. I pirouetted twice, then pliéd. The class applauded. That was all there was to it.

Only during a parent-teacher meeting did my mother find out about this "performance." I remember her saying one of her classic statements—"Well, Nancy~"—as if she was pleased at my courage (or was it audacity?). This would be a common response from her throughout my childhood and adulthood. Mom took pleasure in the times when I stepped outside the norm, took a risk.

IN THE 1880s, the town of Mineral Wells was established because of its waters with so-called "curative powers." The community flourished when people came seeking remedies for various conditions, from insanity to arthritis. We arrived in 1953, and for me, the town came to represent sickness, not healing.

During the first summer, I contracted German measles. Because this condition was dangerous, especially to my eyes, I spent days in a darkened bedroom, listening to 78 rpm records of "Alice in Wonderland" and "Peter Pan."

ENDLESS HOURS PASS as I lie in this dark room. I sweat and itch. The only light is a sliver of sun that comes in around the edge of a curtain. I'm not allowed to read because it might damage my eyes, and when I listen to my stories on records, frightening figures come out of the shadows. One day, Alice sips from the "Drink Me!" bottle and grows too big for the house. Her arms and legs stick out of the doors and windows. Before she drank, she was little like me, but now she's a giant, her large arms and legs, her feet sticking out of the windows and doors of the house. I'm afraid of her because she's so big. Then Captain Hook tries to capture Peter Pan and the boys. Hook's laughter, deep and growly, floats through my bedroom. He sounds like he's right next to me. I'm scared to open my eyes in case I'll see him in my room.

I sweat, and then I shiver. One afternoon I call Mom into the room.

"I see the bear family high on the wall of my bedroom, near the ceiling, Mom. Papa Bear, Mama Bear, and Baby Bear are dancing. Do you see them? Where's Goldilocks?"

The characters of that story run back and forth at the top of my wall. There is no sound, just movement.

I'm sure my mother was frightened by my hallucinations, yet I recall only her steady presence. She bathed my face with cool water, and she brought me juice and chicken noodle soup. As a child, she had measles in her eyes that affected her eyesight for the rest of her life. She was afraid for me though she said nothing about it. I could just tell somehow because she checked on me so often.

I was sick with measles for weeks, and for days after I left behind the hallucinations and the dark room, I had to bathe in calamine lotion to soothe my scabby skin.

DURING ONE of the summers in Mineral Wells, Mom visited a doctor for a lump in her breast. She was scheduled for surgery at a hospital in a distant town, miles from our home, through the desert. Dad, Marge, and I drove to see her one hot afternoon. In the early1950s, few cars had air conditioning. The temperature outside must have been 110 degrees. After several hours of driving through the desert, we finally arrived at the air-conditioned hospital.

As we enter the cool hospital, my stomach turns over. I think I might throw up. Then I see a nurse's uniform. It's very white. The nurse pushes Mom into the room in a wheelchair. My mother looks like someone I don't know. Her white skin blends into the pale white of the waiting room walls and the nurse's uniform. I've never seen Mom look so sick. She's like a ghost and I think maybe she's already dead. In the next minute, the ceiling spins around above me. I know only that my father picks me up, and then all goes black. I wake up in a hospital bed and a nurse offers me chipped ice and a Coke.

The doctor tells us that Mom only has a cyst, so we stop worrying so much about her.

I like it when Daddy holds me. Even if I'm dizzy and sick, I feel safe.

Sometimes Mom will ask, "I don't know why all of you girls want your father's attention, instead of mine." All I know is my sisters and I really want to please Dad.

After all, Mom is always there. Dad's not.

IN DECEMBER OF 1954, we moved to Fort Sill, Oklahoma. For the first time in my life, I felt I was living in a real neighborhood with streets that curved and looped around. I had freedom here. I was old enough to wander out of our yard. Kids rode their bikes up and down and around in circles in front of our house. It felt like the kind of neighborhood I longed for, where I could make friends and we would stay forever.

Marge taught me to ride my bike. I took piano lessons from Mrs. Rodin, a French lady whose husband was in the newly organized Army Air Force. I joined a Brownie troop. I even kept a diary to record the important things that happened: "August 15: The troop met at my house. Mom and Mrs. Blake were there. We baked cookies. Then we ate them."

I felt I belonged at Fort Sill.

I COLLECT LADYBUGS in a jar until my fingertips turned red with the fine dust on their bodies. I find a hairy tarantula on the back porch, and one afternoon I discover a scorpion crawling around in our bathtub. I learn about frogs making babies, and I keep a pail of them in gravel and water. They are the size of a thumbnail. Every day I visit them several times. I take them in my hands and watch their tiny green-brown bodies hop on my palm. I love them so much that I play with them right up to dinnertime. Sometimes I forget to wash my hands before sitting down at the table. One afternoon I find the pail turned over, the gravel and water thrown on the ground, I hurry to pick up the pail, afraid my little friends are dead. They're gone. I never see the frogs again. Though I never find out, I think a mean kid in the neighborhood took them. I hope he didn't kill them.

FORT SILL was one of the last places where Marge and I would live together. Something in me knew she couldn't stay with us forever, but when I thought she might leave, I pushed the thought away. Mom called her my "other mother" because of the way she cared for me after I was born. She was my Santa Claus and my Tooth Fairy, and she brought me light in the darkness of Alaska. I remember when I was very small, she drew funny faces on her clenched fist and made the faces grimace and smile and talk to me. Her limber fingers crept slowly up my arm while she chanted, "Here comes the creep mouse!" until she could goose me on the neck, saying "Gotcha!" She introduced me to my first banana split, urging me to savor the rich flavors of chocolate syrup, strawberry and vanilla ice cream, nuts, bananas, whipped cream, and cherries.

In Fort Sill, my sister and I would lie on a blanket in the afternoon and put our heads in our cupped hands, looking for shapes in the clouds. Once I found a castle and a dinosaur. Marge found a cow. That day she recited "Hey Diddle Diddle."

> *Hey diddle diddle,*
> *The cat and the fiddle,*
> *The cow jumped over the moon,*
> *The little dog laughed to see such fun,*
> *And the dish ran away with the spoon.*

I never understood the poem, but I loved her gentle, animated voice as she said the lines.

ON JUNE 14, 1954, my eighth birthday, my father came home for lunch. Before he reached the porch, I heard some jets above us. I was inside the house and Dad called me out into the warm, clear afternoon, a sky my favorite aqua blue. He pointed up toward the skywriting of the jets—"NANCY!"

In many ways, this incident came to represent the tenor of my father's love for me. What other kid has her name emblazoned in the summer sky? He couldn't speak his love, but he surely could show it.

LATE THAT SUMMER, Dad came home in the middle of the afternoon, earlier than usual, and he looked deflated, his pride gone. Mom and I were both in the front yard, and I was playing with a friend.

"They lost my papers. That son-of-a-bitch Major — probably let the deadline pass deliberately."

I heard Mom gasp.

"I've reenlisted, but I'll only be a master sergeant. I should have known that ass would do everything to ruin my career."

I thought about Dad marching at the front corner of his battalion, his eyes ahead, back straight and tall, his uniform chest and sleeves covered with ribbons from World War II and his service in the Aleutians and New Guinea, and shiny buttons for the Corps of Engineers. His voice always sounded like a commander, a respected man.

This event was probably the most devastating in my father's career. That day, I felt anger growing in my chest. I wanted to hurt the bad people who had hurt my dad.

Now my father spent time in the NCO Club with other non-commissioned officers. When he was home, he spoke little, and instead of telling us tales about his work and his men, he didn't talk about much of anything.

IN THE SPRING OF 1955, a few months after his job change, we found out that Dad had orders to deploy to Korea in July. Mom, Marge and I would move to Houston to live in a rental house across the street from Dad's youngest sister, Ethel, her husband, and their six children. Dad would be gone again, this time for eighteen months. He'd be a long way from us, on the other side of the world. Again, I would have to leave my friends.

Another move. Always another move away from this place where I felt at home.

ONE AFTERNOON after school that spring, I am outside playing marbles with my friend Laura. The block is filled with kids I know from school, riding bikes and playing. I love the beautiful colors of the marbles, especially the cat's eyes, their smooth texture, the feel of them in my palm and between my fingers! Another girl, Suzy, scuffles over to us and asks to play. I don't like Suzy. I can't remember why, but on this day, I want to have control of something, even if it's just a game of marbles.

"You can't play with us. I don't like you." I tell her. Suzy starts crying. I am only faintly aware that a car door has slammed behind me just a moment ago. Dad has just arrived from work, and I'm scared he heard what I said.

My friend and I are sitting on the ground next to the walkway to the house. I am lifted from behind by the arms, and suddenly I am being spanked and spanked again and again. Time halts as I look around and see people are looking. Other kids on the block stop playing to watch. Mom and Margie , who were talking in the living room, come out of the door and stand without saying a word. I think he will never stop hitting me. I am in the open. I feel naked, without shelter. Marge's face turns away from me as she goes inside the house. She looks like she's embarrassed or maybe ashamed for me.

I run in the house, into my bedroom, and slam the door. I cry into my pillow for a long time. I hate my Dad!

He's never hit me before, not one time. A big anger seems to have come over him. He seems madder than I've ever seen him.

The next day, on the way to school in the bus, I overhear two girls giggling. When they see me, they stop laughing, and then

35

whisper, one to the other, "You should have seen her get it." Then they laugh again.

I have always been the good little soldier, one who follows the rules. My teachers write "good student" and "willing worker" on my report cards. "Nancy is the ideal pupil that all teachers appreciate. How we shall miss her!"

Now I'm a failure.

But we never talk about it.

I want to go back to how it was before it happened.

Every time I see a cat's eye marble, my stomach turns over.

I WAS ONLY ABLE to unpack this memory decades later, when I realized that I'd never spoken it or written about it. With all the memories Mom and I discussed in the years following Dad's death, we never talked about this one. It was as if she understood my deep humiliation, knew I wanted to avoid the pain.

She was right.

Finding a Home, Regardless

7

FROM 1955 TO 1957, Dad was deployed to South Korea, where he would stay for eighteen months and construct roads and bridges to facilitate U.S. action in the aftermath of the Korean War. Mom, Marge, and I moved into the rental house across the street from Dad's youngest sister, Ethel, her husband Prentiss, and their six kids. I thought the giant pine trees looked like soldiers who stood alert against the humid, hot air. In the back yard of our house on Chippendale Street, I sat on the grass and worked for hours on geography maps and English lessons. As I drew maps of exotic foreign places, graded with hills and valleys, I wondered how far away Korea was. Where was Daddy?

You'd think that living across from first cousins would be a boon, after all the times I'd left friends behind. It was great, until I had to play rough. The two girls, Sally and Patsy, were closest to my age. Their older brothers Tommy and Jerry were already in high school and college, and the younger ones, Jimmy and Billy were tough little boys, their bodies solid as hard earth. They regularly fought and played tackle ball on their front yard. Patsy and Sally were tomboys. I buried my head in Nancy Drew mysteries and Sue Barton books. They would tease me and call me "scaredy cat" because I didn't like to play rough games with them. One afternoon they tied my wrists to a clothesline and left me captive for over an hour. The clothesline was coated with plastic, but my wrists carried the marks of my captivity for a while afterward.

I tried to fit in as I had in every other place I had lived. I tried to play kick ball with Jimmy, Patsy, and Sally.

One afternoon it's my turn to kick the ball. Jimmy, who is only nine years old but strong as a high school football player, tackles me and I fall down. When his body hits mine, shock waves run through me. We move the game to the street and when I kick the ball, my feet come out from under me and I fall on my back on the concrete. I can't breathe. I'm sure I'm dying. After I crawl from the concrete, I limp to a neighbor's house, the home of a really chubby girl who eats sticks of margarine straight from the wrapper. Her mother tells me, "You'll be fine. Quit crying. Your breath will come back in a few minutes." She gives me a cookie, as if that will help me breathe.

I hate playing rough! Why am I the only one who cries? Maybe I am a scaredy cat!

I go home because I don't feel safe. And I think my cousins are laughing at me.

THERE WERE ALSO many good times with my cousins, especially the girls. We went to the Gulf of Mexico to swim, and we played rummy in Aunt Ethel's and Uncle Prentiss's air-conditioned bedroom. We spent the night at each other's houses. Sometimes Uncle Prentiss teased me, rubbing the skin on my wrist until it felt raw and dirt appeared on the surface. And sometimes I spent the night with Patsy and Sally, or ate dinner with them. I always offered to wash dishes there. It was more fun to help Aunt Ethel than Mom. During those sleepovers, I learned about menstruation and wearing a pad between my legs. I found out that a boy has something like a hotdog between his legs. I remembered Bobby.

Theirs was a lively family, with kids constantly running in and out of the house. I would often see Aunt Ethel burst out of the front door and chase one of the smaller kids with a broom. Uncle Prentiss was a natural-born quick talker, a man who always worked out of the home at who-knows-what business. Words rattled out of his mouth as fast as Morse code. He reminded me of a praying mantis—all legs and arms. A tall, lanky man, he darted around the house most days in Bermuda shorts with a beer in his hand. He named his business enterprise "Acme Company" so that it came early in the phone book. The fact that he never "went to work" seemed natural for him, but it seemed natural that he worked at home. I was with Prentiss when I saw my first $100 bill one afternoon when he stopped for a six-pack of beer on the way to the beach with a carload of kids. That day, he drummed his fingers on the steering wheel to the music of Johnny Cash.

I recall this period of my life whenever I visit a hot, humid climate. It's with Uncle Prentiss that I first heard the music of Johnny Cash.

Walking the Line with Johnny Cash

A hot, humid day near Houston,
driving along a beach white
with sizzling sand. The back seat
of Uncle Prentiss's car is hot enough
to cook an egg, much less my
ten-year-old flesh. A guy on the radio
sings about taking care of his heart.
Cousins Sally and Patsy
and a neighborhood girl,
we are all there in the car with tall
Daddy Prentiss, whose long legs stick up
above the accelerator, knobby knees
reaching upward toward his chest.
He can't ever sit still. His nervous
fingers diddle on the steering wheel,
the dash and the seat beside him.
Windows down, humid air blows
in my face, a headache like

sickness above my eyes, aching pouches
press in, turn my tummy to acid.

The radio keeps blaring that song
about walking the line, about somebody
who couldn't quite trust himself
to do the right thing
with the right person
at the right time.

A promise to be true, a tie that binds,
a voice sounding so hillbilly
that I don't want to hear it, don't want
to like it, don't want to admit it.
I'm enchanted by a regular beat and a voice
that's steady. He talks about simple
things and love, about life and mistakes
and challenges, and about forgiveness,
all to a rhythm that sounds like
the steady beat of big truck tires
on the highway.

After all, I am just ten years old.
All I know about life is that grownups
always seem to know what they are doing
all of the time. But this song, this voice,
this man, here he is singing about being
uncertain, about making mistakes.

On the way home, Uncle Prentiss
stops at a gas station, goes inside to buy
a cold six-pack of Lone Star, long-neck
bottles sweating in the cardboard container.
He pulls out the first 100 dollar bill I've
ever laid eyes on, flashes it quick and crisp
at the guy pumping his gas.

Prentiss gives us some bills,
lets us buy those pop-up popsicles, the ones
you push up through a tube to lick the
red and white and blue sherbet inside. The
cool ice soothes my mouth. The radio plays
that song again, the one about trying to live right,
about making mistakes. Prentiss rolls up
the car windows, turns on the air conditioner,
and we start home.

Hey Mr. Cash, you sure know how to
make that guitar sing!

My headache is gone.
I close my eyes and listen
to the steady rhythm of big truck tires
on the highway.

FOR AWHILE in this Houston suburb, I felt like a normal kid again. At Halloween, Mom dressed like a witch and joined right in with the neighborhood festivities. She sat on Aunt Ethel's front porch, handing out candy. Her low, gravelly voice and her creaky laugh emerged from a dark stole wrapped around her head. The little kids stayed a few feet back, reached quickly to pick Tootsie Rolls or Double Bubble gum from her basket and ran away from the witch's clutch as fast as they could.

Here, I had friends to play with, if I dared risk my life in another game of kickball.

The fifth grade at Forest Park Elementary proved to be a good year for me. I kissed my teacher, Mrs. Simpson, on the cheek every morning as I entered the classroom. Our class learned a Scandinavian dance, and I dressed like a girl from Denmark. I had two boyfriends. Skip's name stayed with me, but the other boy remains nameless, though I remember he was shorter than me and had wavy, brown

41

hair. I had fun at the movies, sitting between them and holding hands with both of them at the same time.

Dad regularly sent home packages, letters, and pictures from Korea. In photos, his camp looked desolate, with road construction backhoes and tractors cluttering the background. As a non-commissioned soldier, he now slept in a plain tent, on an Army cot. The pictures he sent of himself showed him asleep, or reading a book at bedtime, in his long johns. He was there to help maintain the uneasy "peace" after two years of armistice talks ended in 1953. I never remember him speaking about the Korean War itself.

THE DANCING GEISHA GIRL Dad sent me is about two feet tall and is dressed in a kimono of a red and gold threaded pattern. She turns on a revolving platform, moving around slowly to a song. Sometimes when I'm sleeping, I can hear her song, mournful in a minor key.

Every morning when Mom comes to wake me for school, she winds up my Geisha doll. Her melody encircles me like a hug while I'm half awake. I feel sad because Dad is gone. That melody reminds me of him.

Our teacher shows us where Japan and Korea are on the globe. They're all the way on the other side of the world.

Dad is so far away.

29 July 56

Dear Nancy:

How is my little girl getting along this hot weather? Sure am sorry that you did not get to go to Alabama for a while this summer but you have to remember that we always have to take the bitter with the sweet. That is just the way you have to look at all disappointments. Maybe we can go for a few days during your Xmas holidays.

What are you doing this summer? Your mom says you go swimming every day. Bet you sure can swim good now. Can't wait to see how good you are swimming.

Are you taking dancing and piano this summer? Don't try to take much extra work during your vacation because little girls are supposed to rest, play and work in the summer. If the teachers thought it was good for you to study and go to school in the summer, they would not have vacations.

How is Marjorie feeling now. Guess you are helping your mother to take care of her. Be sure to be good and help Marjorie get well quick.

How often do you see Betty, Dwayne and Bub? It must be nice to be able to just walk around the block and be at their house.

Must close.

Love
Dad

PS Will be home before too long.

IN JANUARY 1957, Dad returned home to sit in his stuffed chair and stare into space. Every day was the same. He watched Westerns on our black-and-white television and smoked unfiltered Camels or Chesterfield cigarettes. The smoke rings rolled off his tongue, rose above him, and then disappeared. They left a stale odor.

MARGE WAS LIVING WITH US, working in an office, and dating several guys. She was tall and pretty, and she loved to play tennis and dance. And she included me in her life, even took me on dates with her boyfriends.

43

One night, my sister and I danced in the living room. She put a 78 record of "Blue Tango" on the record player with the dark walnut cabinet. Slowly she moved around the room. She counted *one, two, three, four*, and at the same time she showed me how to make the box with my feet, how to sway at my hips with each second corner. I followed her lead and moved in a square. I felt the beat and learned to sway like she did. One of her boyfriends looked on from the periphery of the room, but to me he wasn't important. Marge was the center of my universe, a mom when mine was unable to be present, and a dad when mine was gone.

While we were in Houston, Marge became ill for the first time with "a nervous disorder." We had no idea what was wrong. She didn't laugh anymore. She wasn't fun the way she'd always been.

MOM, AUNT ETHEL, AND I visit Marge at Anderson Hospital. I'm excited. I haven't seen my sister for several days. When we get off of the elevator, I run ahead to Room 425. I open the door and see Marge in bed. She's so pale she almost disappears against the white sheets, kind of like Mom did that other time in the hospital. I don't understand what's the matter with my sister. I know she has something called shock therapy sessions in the hospital.

We visit for a few minutes, but Mom and Aunt Ethel do most of the talking. Marge just looks at us as if she's not sure why we're here.

When we leave, we stop off at the gift store downstairs. Mom has promised to buy me a pack of miniature playing cards. I was excited about the cards before our visit, but now, I don't really care. I'm scared about Marge.

DAD GOT HIS ORDERS to relocate to Fort Leonard Wood, Missouri. We hadn't heard very good things about it, only that it was a boring place in the sticks. We were supposed to be there by May. I had to leave my friends and my favorite teacher. On my last day of class, they surprised me with a farewell party, with presents. I cried when I left that day. I had just begun to feel at home again.

My greatest sadness was losing Marge, who decided to stay in Houston and live with Betty and Dwayne. She needed to find her own way.

We were headed to "Fort Lost-in-the-Woods," as the soldiers called it.

Tornado Summer

8

BEGINNING IN MAY, 1957, we spent five months at Fort Leonard Wood. The base seemed a kind of purgatory, another wait for Dad's final assignment. As I remember it, the place was stark, desolate. The base seemed flat and dull. Dry, crumbling dirt surrounded us. Mom couldn't even make her petunias grow.

It was as if the rest of the world had turned its back on this base.

In total, I attended only a few weeks of fifth grade and eight days of class at the beginning of the fall school year. As we again prepared to move, my parents received a pink piece of paper from the Waynesville School District. "Nancy has done her assignments successfully, but she has not had enough school to establish grades."

During that summer, Dad applied for the Third Army, Patton's prized military machine. He never heard from them despite his experience in construction and engineering.

WE WON'T BE HERE LONG, so we don't have all of our furniture. Mom calls our house "dinky," too small even to hold her piano or dining set. I sleep on the couch, Dad on a small cot, and Mom on my bed. Finally, when some of the furniture arrives, I get my own room, with a porthole door to the outside. I think about sneaking out at night, but I never do.

I follow the rules. One night after the movies, I refuse to go on a second and third round on the base bus line with the other kids. They get in trouble. I'm praised for being "a good girl," for following the rules.

Yep. This place is "lost in the woods." We have no telephone. When I'm sick at school, the teacher calls the neighbor, who comes to our house and tells Dad to drive to nearby Waynesboro, where my school is located, to pick me up.

EVERY MORNING I ride the school bus down a mountainous road. The bus curves as the road curves, moving in and out of the speckled sunlight that shows through the dense forest.

One morning, we hear that a tornado has leveled some of the base housing where we live in the non-commissioned officers' neighborhood. The houses are fragile dwellings that look like so many square disposable cans, "cracker box houses," my mother calls them, not strong enough to resist the might of a tornado. I think of my room, the porthole door flying off, all of my clothes and books ripped from the house by winds.

A greenish-yellow sky covers the school like a warm blanket soggy with rain. It's like a curtain, or a mask that clings to my face so close that when I breathe, I am breathing water, almost drowning. Winds blow with fury, deafening winds crying and moaning. Trees sway, then comes a cracking sound—branches tear off and fly away, out of sight. Then quiet, and menacing, heavy air surrounds us.

This quiet is scary. The heavy air holds still, waiting for something. The winds start again, furious, and then I hear a roaring like a train over us. How can a train be so close by, sounding like it's passing above our heads?

The teachers hurry us downstairs to the basement cafeteria. We crouch under long cafeteria tables, listen to the wind and rain whip the sides of the building. I clutch a small brass decal with the Catholic version of The Lord's Prayer printed on it. *It will protect me.* But I'm scared, afraid that a tornado has hit our house. *Mom and Dad are dead. I just know it.*

While I'm kneeling under the table, I think of Dad's story from his youth, the night at dinner when he and his parents, his brother and sisters heard the sound of a train near the house. To them it seemed different from the train that regularly ran through Hartselle. This one was louder, closer, more intense. Soon the winds picked up and a tornado passed over the house, leaving tree limbs and boards strewn over the property. Outside, the family surveyed the damage. They heard their cow mooing, but only after a search did they find her high in a tree in a nearby yard.

I never heard him say how they got the cow down. I didn't care. I just loved the funny story.

Today, though, tornadoes aren't funny.

How could the winds have so much power? I curl up deeper under the cafeteria table, grasping my knees and holding them to my chest, still clutching my "Our Father" decal.

The storm passes, we return to class, and at the end of the day, we ride home on the bus. I find Mom and Dad aren't hurt and our house is okay too, but for a long time I remember the sound of rushing wind, the sickly green of the sky as the twister passed over our school.

The tornado is kind of like our lives. Many nights I go to bed afraid of the least wind or rain. I clasp that brass decal in my hand tightly until The Lord's Prayer is imprinted on my palm.

I need something, or someone, to make me feel safe.

ALTHOUGH LEONARD WOOD represented the limbo before Dad's final assignment in Sault Ste. Marie, Michigan, I still attempted to put down roots. I couldn't help myself. I had learned to be a chameleon, changing colors with every environment. I just needed to figure out what color to change to.

It didn't take me long to make friends. *I can do this again,* I told myself. *I can belong.* That summer I attended the base chapel's Bible

School and went to the movies and the pool with other kids on the base. With my best friend Rayann, I sewed doll clothes for my Jenny doll, and we danced in my small living room to Elvis' "You Ain't Nothing but a Hound Dog." This was at the peak of the Cold War angst, and I saw *Tarantula*, a movie about a hairy spider that grew to 300 feet as the result of scientific experimentation gone awry (I remembered my Oklahoma back porch visitor). I saw *The Creature from the Black Lagoon*, about a gilled creature that stood erect, like a man, and carried the leading lady to his cave. For months afterward, I had dreams that I was in love with the creature. He was carrying me into the deep tunnels of his lagoon.

Perched on the edge of puberty, I became friends with an African American boy, Joey, the son of another soldier. One day Dad told me the hard truth about being friends with the boy. "People might get the wrong idea." Did he mean because I was a girl, people would think we were misbehaving? Or was he talking about the boy's color? Dad had spent time with black soldiers, taken one black friend to his parents' home for lunch, and rejected the segregation policies of the country. It didn't make sense to me at the time.

I understand better today, in the context of history. Two years before that conversation about the black boy, in 1955, the Civil Rights Movement had been launched by Rosa Parks' refusal to sit at the back of a bus in Montgomery, Alabama. But it would be six years before the Civil Rights Act passed in Congress. Racial tension was rising.

Dad must have known the culture we would encounter once we returned "home" to Alabama after his retirement. Now I think he was preparing me for the racism I'd find.

WE HAD BROUGHT our part-Persian cat Taffy with us from Houston, where she lived both in and out of doors. She's the only cat I know who had a broken tail from catching it in a screen door. The poor cat looked funny when she dragged her splinted tail across the floor. Mom complains about her wailing in her cage or trying to get free from the leash she wears outside, tied to the clothesline. It's orders from headquarters: "No pets can run loose on base."

I feel like Taffy—tied up. But I don't wail. I keep quiet. Neither Taffy nor I like moving, but we do it anyway. When we packed in Houston, she hid herself for hours before Mom found her closed up in a trunk. On our last day in Leonard Wood, she disappears while we wait in our car crammed with suitcases, books, and Taffy's cage and litter box.

Dad calls the MPs. "Our cat, a blonde Persian, has disappeared. We're trying to get out of here. Can you look for her?"

They put out a base-wide alert to try to find her.

Mom says, "We'll just have to leave her. We can't wait all day."

She sounds impatient.

"No, Mom, we can't leave her! She's my cat!" I'm about to cry when the soldiers arrive with Taffy in hand. They look funny, with their stiff uniforms, buttons and patches, the "MP" on their hats, guns on their belts, and fluffy cat in the arms of one of the soldiers.

Dad doesn't suggest leaving Taffy. He seems to understand.

Leaving the Army

9

DAD'S LAST ASSIGNMENT was Sault Ste. Marie, Michigan. Located at the northern border of the Upper Peninsula of Michigan, it's called "the Soo" by the locals. Everywhere is evidence of the history of Chippewa Indians, French fur traders, and skirmishes between the French and British. The Soo is the third oldest settlement in the United States. We arrived in 1957, when I was eleven, and it still reflected the diverse European groups that had arrived earlier. The local industry at the time was Union Carbide. The most distinctive feature of this little port town was the International Locks. Freighters used them to move from Lake Superior to the other Great Lakes because of a twenty-one-foot drop from Superior to the lower water levels of other lakes.

I immediately loved the international flavor of the place, its worldliness. Sailors from around the world frequented the bars and restaurants along the channel. It was risky for a young girl to walk about alone, especially at night.

Dad gave me strict instructions to look straight ahead, avoiding the gaze of men who might be looking at my barely burgeoning young body. "This town can be rough," he said. To me, rough meant much more exciting and less safe than the Army bases where we had lived before.

A sixteen-year-old guy from my seventh-grade class often stood on the corner downtown wearing his leather jacket and tight jeans. I don't recall his name, but his hair was oiled and combed into a duck tail. One day in class, our teacher Mrs. Sharp, a tiny woman, under five-feet tall, told him to be quiet. He stood up, knocked her to the floor, and left the classroom. Mrs. Sharp got up and went on writing on the blackboard as if nothing had happened. We sat stunned in our desks. No one said a word. I wondered if she was hurt.

The "hood," as we called him, was on the corner most times when I went down by the locks. He frightened me and I looked straight ahead, never acknowledging him.

THERE WERE MANY CHARMS in this exotic little town. One was ice skating. I first tried to skate on our neighbor's little ice rink in her yard. When I fell flat on my stomach, my front tooth pierced my lower lip and it bled. Yet I learned to love skating despite being very slow and off balance, wobbly. On Saturdays my best friend Carla and I would visit the town skating rink, looking for boys. Sometimes I saw Jody there, or Adam.

I was in love with both of them at the same time. Jody was the blond basketball player. Adam was a handsome boy in our class who looked like James Dean. One night at a party, I stood in the corner talking with Jody for a long time. There was a fire in the fireplace close by. We danced to the Platters' song "Only You," and I smelled his clean aftershave, felt his lean body against mine. I had an ache, a longing in my stomach and my chest. I was only thirteen and had not bled yet. I didn't understand my body, but I felt the same ache at night when I lay in my small bed below the eaves of the green house, listening to Bobby Darin or Frankie Valle for hours after Mom and Dad were asleep. It was a kind of yearning that made my heart ache while my tears ran down my cheeks onto my pillow.

Now I know this was the beginning of puberty and the transference of my need for Dad onto my need for a boyfriend.

The ache I felt was both loneliness and longing as I envisioned the beautiful women in the novels I read at night. They were wrapped in the arms of their handsome men, who were always brave and valiant. Of course, I was not one of these beautiful women, but I wanted— ached—to be in those stories.

In seventh grade, I was a plain-looking kid, a square who studied all the time when I wasn't thinking about boys. I would never be like Connie, a cheerleader who wore her blond hair in a ponytail. I was chubby and had large front teeth (sometimes kids call me "Bucky"). And I was an outsider. Because my dad was the National Guard Army Advisor, I was different. Most of the kids had lived in Sault Ste. Marie for a while and their fathers worked in the community, like my best friend Carla's dad, who worked at Union Carbide. These friends had roots. They belonged.

I did find some consolation for being in this "foreign" place. After we left Alaska, since we'd lived in Texas and Oklahoma, we had seen no snow at all. Mom and I had longed for it. Now we had it, more than enough. I would go with Dad to the old city library where he checked out Zane Grey novels and I devoured Dr. Doolittle books and historical romances. Those times were special for me— times when just Dad and I did something together, just the two of us. I can still smell the musty odor of old books, their hard, slick covers gleaming in the stacks. Sometimes the covers were plastic, sometimes leather. The Dr. Doolittle books had colorful sketches of the doctor and his animals on the covers, and I remember from one of them a picture of a butterfly in marmalade.

These times with Dad stand out in contrast to the moments of loneliness and failure I often felt when I was around him.

My parents and I, along with our cat Taffy, lived in a house painted forest green. First, we lived in the upstairs apartment, where I had the attic bedroom under the eaves. Later, we moved downstairs. I invited my friends over for dance parties, the furniture in our small living room pulled out to the edges of the room so we could move on the wood floors to "Johnny Angel" and "I'm Mr. Blue." Late into the night, beneath the protecting eaves in my loft bedroom, I would read the exotic romance novels about women being captured by handsome natives and stolen away into the jungle.

Because being in love seemed important, I longed for Jody and Adam, just as I longed for Dad's attention.

In the back yard of the green house, I practiced my tennis serve against the side of the old garage and pitched softballs with my dad. I played on a girls' softball team. Dad had been a star baseball player in college, and my sister Marge had been a strong, fast ball player, yet I had trouble with every aspect of the game. Day after day, we pitched balls in the yard, Dad telling me about the angle of my arm, the arch of the ball. Time after time, I threw a slow curve or failed to watch the ball carefully enough. As my parents sat in the bleachers one summer afternoon, I struck out twice and missed two fly balls in left field.

I was humiliated, for me and for them. On the way home, no one spoke. I felt like a failure.

During a dance in our church basement, I finally figured out why I tried so hard at softball. The minister divided the girls and boys into pairs. That night I was the extra girl and had to lead. "Anyway, Nancy, your dad wanted a boy the last time," he said.

Did the preacher know something I didn't?

Dad never told me I was a disappointment. In fact, in this last phase of his military career he didn't say much. If he wasn't at the Armory, he was silent, drinking wine and watching television in the living room.

One afternoon after school I asked him something. I don't remember what. I probably just wanted to connect with him. He slumped in his chair in the living room, a small juice glass and wine bottle, his Chesterfields and an ashtray half-filled with cigarette butts on the table next to him. I said something again. I heard only a moan and it frightened me. I found Mom in the kitchen, washing dishes.

"Mom, something's wrong with Dad. I don't know who he is, Mom. Where's my Dad?" I don't remember what she said to me. It was as if I was back in West Lafayette, Indiana, when Dad stumbled around or had to be carried to bed.

After that I escaped to my bedroom, where I listened to the radio and tried to forget my daddy was not really there.

One Saturday I asked Dad to take me to the hardware store. I needed some wood, screws, and wiring to make an electric motor for an extra-credit science project. I had a crush on my science teacher. I wanted to impress him with my smarts, like my classmate Janet did.

Two times I asked Dad to take me to the store. He didn't respond, just sat and watched TV. Finally, after a third time, he sighed, rose from his chair slowly, like an old man, and drove me to the store. I felt guilty because I was bothering him. I should have left him alone.

I worked for hours on that motor. I was challenged and excited. Maybe I could make this thing! Working with the wiring, I twisted and folded it into shapes to fit the sketch in my science book. My fingertips grew sore and smelled like metal. The end result resembled a hillbilly shack, the splintered wood sticking out at odd angles.

I turned in my assignment to my science teacher on Monday, but even he couldn't make my motor work.

Mom praised me for trying to build it in the first place. Dad never mentioned the motor.

Despite disappointments, I just had to bring home all "As," I thought. My teacher wrote on a report card that I didn't finish assignments on time. "I think it is because she wants it perfect in every detail." I had a steady record of As and Bs, with an occasional C in Physical Education or Home Economics. Somehow, I knew I would never be a scientist or a tidy housewife. I knew I loved music and literature.

These were my mother's passions. I can remember always feeling that she was there, along with her love of the arts. I didn't realize then that she had put aside her passions for her marriage, but she never let go of them. They were who she was. And she was there for me.

Unlike Dad, who spent most of his time at the Armory, where he seemed most alive and cheerful. It was only a block away, so sometimes I would drop in. Most often, he was laughing, chugging a beer or joking with the men in his company. Only now do I understand the importance of this last military job. If Dad's position as Army Advisor gave him no high rank or power, it did give him responsibility in his advisory role. The men liked him. The Armory was more home to him than our little apartment in the green house.

I HAD A CHANCE to explore the reasons behind my aching chest and belly when I met Jim. He was sandy-haired, an "older guy" of fifteen. He'd been around. He knew the rough side of town.

Jim took me to an Eagle Scout dance one night. He walked to my house after dark. When Dad told him to be sure to protect me, Jim pulled a knife out of his pocket to show him.

As we got to know each other, Jim asked me to come to his house while his parents worked, when only he and his sister were at home.

Many afternoons we lay on the floor in his living room. We kissed, and I felt his hands moving down my back toward my bottom. He never put his hands under my clothes, but he stroked my back and we kissed a long time. I knew this was wrong, that it went against my church teaching, but I was curious. After an hour or so, we'd sit up, straighten our clothes, and he would walk me home. Mom and Dad never asked what I'd been doing. Later, I lay in my loft bedroom, the slanted ceiling beams close to my face. I thought of my friend Ann, who had an older boyfriend who came to her house at night. She had no father, and her mother let her boyfriend stay, sometimes until early the next morning. I wondered what they did all night.

I don't understand why Jim never groped under my clothes. Maybe I stopped him. Maybe I didn't respond. But he did give me a silver heart with "Jim" inscribed on one side and "Nancy" on the other. I still have it.

ONE AFTERNOON in early September 1958, my mother picked up the phone to hear the voice of Rob, my sister Marge's husband. He called Mom by her nickname.

"Bee, Marge is ill. You and Nancy need to come to Houston."
He didn't ask us. He told us. He knew we'd come without question.
By the next day, Mom and my oldest sister Betty had made plans for
me to transfer from my eighth-grade class to Landrum Junior High
in Spring Branch, a suburb of Houston, near Betty's house. The
seeds of Marge's sickness planted years earlier had broken through
the soil. We only knew then that she was not well, often tired and
depressed, but we didn't know the cause.

Mom and I boarded a Greyhound bus to ride from Sault Ste.
Marie. We would change buses in more cities than I can remember.
Since our town was so far north in Michigan, and we would be on
the road to Houston for days. We would travel the full length of the
country.

I didn't want to leave Dad, my cat Taffy, my friends, or Jim. But
that day, as always, what *I* wanted was not important. Mom and I
pulled out of the Sault Ste. Marie station on a bus headed south
toward the Lower Peninsula. Dad stood watching us. I turned to
look at him as he grew smaller and smaller. I missed him already. My
chest ached, and I had a lump in my throat.

For three days and four nights we rode on Greyhound buses,
swaying and lurching, my stomach moving back and forth between
nausea and grinding hunger. Every day, I longed for a bath, an
unmoving, horizontal bed. I longed to breathe fresh air, not the fumes
that spit out of the buses' tail pipes we encountered in every bus stop
and change we made over the endless journey. One afternoon when
I was finally able to sit down with a meal of chicken and spinach in
some town or another, a voice screamed over the loudspeaker, "Bus
number ___ departs in five minutes. Five minutes." There would be
no other connection for six hours. "Five minutes, bus number ___."
We left our food and rushed to the departure area.

We finally arrived at the Houston bus terminal in the middle
of the night. The station was deserted, except for a man in ragged
clothes lying on a bench, snoring. Marge and Rob were nowhere to
be seen. We waited for over a half-hour in the waiting room that
smelled of wet clothes, sweat, and nicotine. When they arrived,

Marge's face was as blank as a white field of snow. "Hi, Nancy," she whispered. That's all she said.

What's happened to her? She's supposed to be happily married. I remembered the black and white photos from her wedding to Rob, her tailored suit and pillbox hat. The bride and groom gazed into each other's eyes, and Marge's dimples showed.

Now, something was definitely wrong, and it frightened me. Like the silence that lurked around Dad, her illness was a menace ready to spring on us. No one talked about it.

Rob was out of work. All four of us moved into Betty and Dwayne's small, square, three-bedroom house in suburban Spring Branch. Three families in a small space. Betty's six-year-old son Dwayne had been diagnosed with rheumatic fever and was staying home from school.

Mom and I lived in a small bedroom where every night I struggled to catch up to my classmates in my new school. My English classmates were ahead of me in grammar—gerunds were foreign and frightening territory. English had always been my strongest subject, but when the report cards came, I had flunked it.

How awful that was! I had a mom who had studied and loved English. She had taught it for one year. I had always made As in English. To fail an English test felt like the real bottom of a jar I was in. I was trapped in a family situation beyond my control, like the lightening bugs I had captured at Mama and Papa Steve's house in Alabama. The difference was I had let the lightening bugs go free, free to light up their little lamps in the darkness. At this point, I had no lamp to light.

I missed my girlfriends, Jim, and the cold weather in the Soo. I especially missed Dad.

[Fall, 1958]

Dear Daddy,

How have you been lately and how is Taffy? I had a long holiday. Got off Thursday and Friday so with the weekend I had a pretty long holiday.

I think this last six weeks has been about the hardest in my life. I would come home, change clothes, & eat a snack. Then I would work sometimes until 10:30 stopping only to eat supper. I was tired all the time.

My work paid off, though. I got a 94 in my Science Six Weeks test, a 98 in my Social Studies Six Weeks test and a 85 in my English 6 Weeks Test. I sure was happy. I don't know about my Math 6 Weeks Test yet. We get our Report Cards next week.

I am in my school newspaper this time. I will explain about it to you. Even though I wasn't here our class had the most subscriptions for the paper so we got our pictures in it. Some of us wrote to the paper things about ourselves. I wrote in and told them how I came here on the bus from Michigan. They make funny things up about what we write. That is why they said that about me.

I have to go now.

Love Always,
Nancy

ONE EVENING, everything exploded at dinner time.

Dwayne came home from work tired. His job at Detrick's Oil Refinery took a toll on him. The heat and challenge to his body aggravated his arthritis. On this night he grabbed a beer and sat down stiffly on the couch in the family room, next to the kitchen.

Tonight, Texas chili was on the stove and sweet cornbread in the oven.

"Marge, would you mind setting the table?" Betty asked. Marge and Rob sat there on the living room couch, his arm around her shoulders. She stared at the floor and didn't move. Dwayne walked into the living room.

"You can't live here and not help," Dwayne yelled.

His voice frightened me. I had to defend my sister.

"Don't yell at Margie! She's sick. Can't you see that?" It came out of my mouth before I realized it.

"Move out. All of you. Now!" Dwayne's yell rose to a scream.

The next day Rob, Marge, Mom and I moved into a duplex near my school. We didn't communicate with Betty and Dwayne for weeks. In our small and shabby apartment, I slept on a bunk bed in the kitchen. Here I bled for the first time one morning, and cried for Dad. My stomach hurt and I was sad.

"I miss Dad," I told Mom.

"Don't say it so loud. Don't tell Marge and Rob you want to go home," Mom whispered. She wanted my silence.

I will be silent and carry my new womanhood quietly. I will be like Marge. She's the most wonderful woman in the world. She hurts but she doesn't talk about it. So can I.

I can recreate the longing I felt for Dad even now, more than fifty years after his death. It was a longing for the goodness in him, his gentleness and the love he had for Mom. I longed for that father, the one I'd seen during our trips to the library, the one who laughed and told stories about growing up in a small town in Alabama, the one who paid attention when I told him my news, the things that worried me. I wanted the father who, in his letters, wrote that Taffy, our cat, had become the company mascot for the Michigan 1437th Engineer Company, that she sat at the table with the soldiers while they ate their meals.

I wanted that father. My hormones were raging, and I felt frightened and vulnerable. Unsafe.

We received frequent letters from Dad. He sent me $10 for Christmas, and a few days later came another package with a small radio for me and a sweater for "Missy," as he sometimes called Mom, that I was supposed to wrap. I went through the motions of Christmas shopping at the five-and-dime store with my friend Lena, who lived next door, finding gifts for my mom, Marge, and Rob, and Dad. And a silver bracelet for Jim. I wasn't very excited about this holiday. In the best years, our family had risen early to open presents, then enjoy a breakfast of fried eggs, ham or bacon, and Mom's fresh biscuits with butter and syrup. The Christmas treat was a half a grapefruit with a maraschino cherry in the middle of it.

Here we were, Mom and I, with Marge and her husband, he out of work, no tree, and most of all, no Dad.

ON CHRISTMAS DAY, Mom and I drove with Marge and Rob to the small town of Mena, Arkansas, where Rob's mother ran a motel and restaurant. It was dark and wet in those Ozark Mountains. The tall pine trees loomed over us as we drove along the winding two-lane mountain road by the motel. Along the way, Rob and Marge joked about breaking the slats of one of the double beds when they slept there before. Mom talked, but I didn't say much. I didn't feel well.

I couldn't eat anything. Was it a stomach virus, or was I homesick for Dad? By afternoon, I still was unable to eat dinner in Ruth's small kitchen, attached to the motel office. I cried. I wanted to be hungry. After all, it was Christmas. But Dad was so far away.

Outside the motel office door, the light of the "closed" sign reflected on the wet road.

DURING THESE MONTHS in Houston, no one spoke of Marge's illness, mostly because we didn't know what it was. But a quiet, troubled feeling lingered around us daily, both at Betty's house and in the cramped duplex. I was silent, as I was supposed to be. So was Mom. It was as if we were just there, waiting. We served no real purpose that I can think of.

By January 1960, we were back in Sault Ste. Marie. As excited as I was when Mom told me we would go back to Michigan, as much as I missed my life there, everything was changed. I returned to school, entering the eighth-grade class. While I was gone, Jim had found another girlfriend who no doubt would lie on his living room floor and let him touch her. And nothing else was the same for me.

I was angry and sad. I don't think I really blamed anybody. Why should I? It was always like this. I had to go wherever I was told to go, whenever the orders came.

Back in the Soo, nothing was the same for me. The spell was broken. I went to a school dance in my special black taffeta dress with a sash of rainbow colors. I came home early, after only a few minutes. I told Mom and Dad that I was not well. I really did feel sick to my stomach. I didn't want to stand around waiting for someone to ask me to dance.

Dad's thirty-year military career ended in spring of 1960, when he was called to Lansing, the state capital, for a retirement ceremony. On the front page of the *Soo Evening News*, a photo shows a waist-high image of Dad, Mom, and me standing together in a line facing a man in uniform. Dad is raising his right hand to take a pledge. Mom and I stare at the commanding officer as if we're at attention. My mother wears one of those '50s women's hats that grips her skull and is decorated with a bit of net. My head is coiffed in its usual boyish haircut, like a soldier's, a hairstyle I will abandon years later, after Dad's death.

Soon we would go home to Alabama.

Leaving Sault Ste. Marie was more difficult than leaving the other places where we'd lived. During our three years there, Mom and I often walked down by the St. Mary's River and stood on the bridge over the rapid waters. We'd watch big freighters go through the locks. Once we waited for hours to see the *Queen Mary*, Queen Elizabeth II's ship, as it found harbor on the Canadian side of the St. Mary's River. Queen Elizabeth was on her coronation tour.

Dad had complained greatly about the weather. "No human being should live in a place like this," he growled as he shoveled snow or brushed it off his car. Yet I could tell he would miss his men. It was not his way to talk about his feelings. Now I can understand that he was sad to leave the Army, a calling he held as sacred as the call of God.

On the morning we drove out of the Soo for the last time, an instrumental version of "Canadian Sunset" played on the radio. My mother fought back tears. My silent father was silent, no doubt already missing his men.

That Old Time Religion

10

IN OUR NEW "HOME" of Alabama, I was like Taffy, a cat on a leash, pulling one direction, then the other, against the controlling forces of the Church and of a small town where my family had settled generations before.

Though the hold of these forces on my life felt strong, the cord would break soon after my father died.

Alabama represented home to both of my parents, but after we arrived, out of habit I expected to move again after a year or two. The rhythm was set in my body, my brain, my spirit. Instead, this time, we put down roots. My parents bought their first and only house on Short Street in Hartselle.

We fell easily into the pattern of the Nelson family churchgoers whose lives were shaped by the Bible. At that time, the Methodist Church was a red brick structure built in the 1920s under the leadership of my grandfather, Steve Nelson, and other men on the building committee. Nancy and Robert Owen, my great-grandparents, attended this church, and when we moved back, we were the third and fourth generations of Nelsons to cast shadows on this church door every Sunday morning, Sunday night, and Wednesday evening for prayer meeting or choir rehearsal.

I was obsessed with my soul's salvation. I read the Bible every day, prayed in the morning and at night, and followed a Bible-reading guide. I read novels like Thomas Costain's *The Silver Chalice* that pulled me back to biblical times. I had bought the 45-rpm record of Tennessee Ernie Ford's hymns as a gift for Dad. On Sunday mornings while we were getting ready for Sunday school, our house rang with Ford's voice:

> *There were ninety and nine that safely lay in the shelter of the fold.*
> *But one was lost on the hill far away, far off from the gates of gold…*

I was determined not to be that lost sheep, though I was convinced that my soul was foul.

I can see Dad listening to Ford's voice, dressed in a suit and tie as he ate his breakfast and looked over his notes for the Adult Sunday School class he taught. He believed those words.

My devotion to Jesus followed me everywhere I went. One day in high school with my two best friends, Pam and Donna, I decided to set up an altar in an empty classroom. My friends were both Baptists, Donna's father a preacher. The three of us decided that the students should have a quiet place to play. We asked the principal if we could recreate a little chapel, and he thought it a good idea. We found an unused classroom and hung velvet curtains on the side of a bench that was just high enough for kneeling. We put a table behind the bench and set a Bible on top, open to the John 3:16, "God so loved the world…"

A few days later, I visited the praying room. The door was open a crack, the room in disarray. The curtains were on the floor, dusty with footprints. The table was turned over, the bench pushed aside. The Bible was gone.

Why don't they see that everybody needs Jesus? I gathered up the dusty drapes while I forced back tears.

DONNA AND HER PARENTS lived outside of town, in a house beside their church, just where the road curves to lead out into the country. When I visited Donna, her dad always chanted, "Praise the Lord!" in a voice that sounded like he was in was in his pulpit, preaching sin and damnation. One afternoon I visited Donna for some private time with her, probably to talk about boys. As he passed through the room, he stopped to ask, "What is the state of your soul, Nancy?"

My stomach tied in knots; I could feel the warmth of my flushed face. *It must be my sin that's making me feel this way. Every morning, I wake up to my stained self. I am not a good person. I will never live up to the perfection of being a Christian.*

Now talking about boys felt sinful and superficial.

On most occasions, Donna's parents broke into our phone conversations every time we talked longer than five minutes. "Donna, it's time to get off the phone." When I heard the extension receiver lifted, I had a lump in my throat and stomach, angry that Donna had no privacy. Her parents hovered close by.

I also couldn't understand why her dad drowned a litter of kittens in a paper bag and in a nearby pond.

How can her father be so holy and kill sweet little kittens?

MY FATHER had a Methodist lay preacher's license, though he couldn't give communion. The lay preacher tradition dates back to John Wesley and the origins of the Methodist Church in England. Sometimes on a Sunday, he preached at a rural church. Mom and I would accompany him. The folks in these small rural churches always appreciated his visit, since they didn't have a regular preacher.

We drove through the country past cotton fields, down dusty roads to these simple, weathered churches.

As my father led the service, the country women, women with faded cotton housedresses and bonnets with calico blinders covering the sides of their faces, would gaze up at him. The men, dressed in overalls and plaid shirts, would listen, barely moving in their seats. They respected Mr. Nelson because he was smart, and to them, he was *blessed*. At those times, like the times he led his battalion, I was proud to be his daughter. When Dad was in the pulpit, he was transformed, as he appears in one photo of him preaching in a chapel pulpit while still an Army officer. His right hand is raised toward his audience, and his face is open wide with a smile that looks like joy.

On regular Sundays, Dad taught the adult Sunday school class. Mom and I sang in the church choir, directed by my Uncle Skinny. In the choir loft behind and elevated above the preacher, we sang hymns and songs arranged for four-part harmony. We wore wine-colored robes, but in summer, they weighed heavy on our shoulders. Aunt Louise, Dad's older sister, played the organ. Sitting to our left, her white head bent over her hands, her fingers played the melody while her little feet tapped matching chords on the pedals.

We were the perfect Christian family.

Hymns about redemption and submission—"Rock of Ages," "When I Survey the Wondrous Cross," "Bringing in the Sheaves," "Why Not Tonight?"— reinforced my sinfulness and need for redemption. "Our relationship with the Lord is personal," said the preacher, "not separate from us like the god of the Catholics who worship idols—statues of the saints and the Virgin Mary. In fact, our relationship with the Lord is like a relationship of a wife to her husband, or a son to his father."

I must give total commitment and service to Jesus. Only then will God take me in holiness. The words about submission to Jesus are the same words I've heard about marriage. Submit to your husband. Give yourself over to him.

We often visited the Tabernacle Revival Campground, which was already over sixty years old at that time. During the summer, our youth group and adult members of the church attended the revivals. A recent *Hartselle Enquirer* reports that the Tabernacle has kept the same schedule for decades: 7:00 a.m., breakfast; 7:30 a.m., Bible study; 10:30 a.m., preaching; 12:00 noon, lunch; 2:30 p.m. preaching (Sunday only); 5 p.m., dinner; 7:00 p.m., choir practice; 7:30 p.m. preaching.

I was my holiest at the Tabernacle Revival.

During the services, the preacher's voice rang out: "Do you want to be cleansed by the blood of the Lamb?"

One night I watched as people left their chairs and traipsed down the aisle to the altar while we're singing.

> *Just as I am, without one plea,*
> *But that thy blood was shed for me.*

I knew that one well. It was about a bad person being forgiven.

An old woman with no teeth and a cane struggled down the aisle. Her son, whose huge belly hung over his belt, helped her kneel at the altar, tears making crevices down his sun-toughened face. Another fellow walked forward. I recognized him from the feed store downtown. His overalls were light blue from too many washings. His plaid shirt was ironed and starched, but sweat soaked wide circles under his arms.

The preacher's voice rose and fell. I felt an urgency, like his family must have felt to hear Noah—"Board the ark quickly! The rains are coming." That night I believed that the only road, the *only* way to salvation was through a personal relationship with Jesus.

If it's true, why don't I feel anything?

I pushed up from my chair and walked forward slowly. I was expecting tears that never came. I tried to cry as I approached the portable altar, assembled for the campground services, but all I knew was that I was hot and wanted to get out of that tent.

I've got to be sure that I'm saved before it's too late. What's the matter with me? Even if I don't really believe it, I know I ought to.

After the preacher prayed over us, we sang a verse or two of another gospel hymn, "There is a Fountain." It was one of my favorites. Mom told me she sang it in her Primitive Baptist church when she was growing up:

> *There is a fountain filled with blood*
> *drawn from Immanuel's veins,*
> *and sinners washed beneath that flood*
> *lose all their guilty stains.*

I hoped my soul was cleansed with the blood of the Lamb. I hoped I was pure.

LATE IN HER LIFE, when my mother entered a nursing home, she gave me my father's hand-written Sunday school lessons. As I read through the tattered pages, some notes are written in pen, some in black ink, some in red, I find a very different religious man than the one I thought I knew. I find that my father was a Gnostic, one who believes that the true power of faith comes from within, not from the outside. In his own words, taken from a lesson: "No one will ever grow in Christian life through the use of the Bible as a sacred relic....We must understand the Bible as a real book written by real people in a real historical situation over a period of several hundred years. Studied critically."

Why didn't I talk with my father about my guilt, my sense of inadequacy? Perhaps I could have listened more to him when he talked with Mom about his lessons. Perhaps I could have asked him questions.

For some reason, I just couldn't reach out to him.

First Wedding

11

IT'S JULY 16, 1966, the summer between my sophomore and junior years at Birmingham-Southern . The sultry Alabama heat presses into the brick walls of the air-conditioned First Methodist Church in Hartselle. Heat rises up from the concrete sidewalk and porch. A slight breeze rustles the trees, but the air is too heavy to make a difference. For this forever first wedding, I wear a traditional wedding dress borrowed from a cousin, with a high lace neck and crinoline petticoats. The dress is stiff and scratchy, and my girdle binds me in as if it had bones laced into the cloth. I've seen this kind of dress in bridal magazines, and I've dreamed of wearing one. As a little girl, I dressed my cat Taffy in a bridal dress and veil from one of my larger dolls and married her to my teddy bear. I don't think she liked it much, judging by her expression in her "wedding photo." She looked trapped, uncomfortable, desperate.

The large Methodist sanctuary, softened by white molding at the top of the light blue walls, is half-filled with friends of the family, my future husband Henry's friends from college and high school, my sorority sisters, and my sisters and their children. Dad and I wait for the bridal music played by my Aunt Louise. We will not hear the "Bridal Chorus" from Wagner's *Lohengrin* because Henry's Anglican priest says Wagner's opera is pagan. Instead, we walk down the aisle to Pachelbel's *Canon in D Major*. With my left arm through his right, I feel the thinness of Dad's limb. Two years earlier he shattered his right elbow after a fall headfirst down basement stairs at my step-grandmother Big Mama's house. That Sunday he opened what he thought was the bathroom door and catapulted to the cement floor below. While falling, he threw up his right arm to shield his face and head. He had surgery, and now his right arm was shorter than his left.

During the service, my friend and high school choral director, Bill, sings, "Entreat me Not to Leave Thee," lyrics from the *Book of Ruth*.

I hear muffled coughing and whispers among the audience. I think my sisters are crying, but I don't turn around to look.

At the altar my betrothed gazes at me with a wide, childish grin, his hair slicked back like a little boy whose mother combed it for him. Henry's eyes gleam behind thick glasses, and with his slight build, he carefully measures every movement he makes.

In front of us, the Methodist preacher wears a simple black robe while the priest dons the colorful gown and cassock of the High Church Anglican.

This marriage will last my lifetime. I am pleasing my family, finding some roots for myself. Whatever happens, it must work. I'll be just like Marge.

In our motel room that night, I wear a white, filmy negligee. As I leave the bathroom where I have changed clothes, Henry stands back to inspect my body, which shows through the gauzy material. His face looks satisfied, as if he's buying a thoroughbred horse.

"How lucky I am." His words are like pieces of ice on my body, like I'm being inspected, naked, watched. His penis swells, rises up in front of him, points at me. I have never seen an erection before.

Earlier in the summer, my very thick hymen was surgically removed. During my first pelvic exam, the doctor said it would tear on penetration and I would bleed profusely.

Dad wants to make sure Henry knows I'm pure. "Nancy, tell Henry about the surgery. He needs to know you are a virgin. It's important."

71

Now on our first night in bed Henry rides over me, and I try to think of other things. Anything but this silly rocking and groaning. *I thought it was going to be magical!*

During this long night, I wake up several times. I have nightmares and dream of horses. I scream, "Help me!" Henry shakes me awake.

The next morning at the motel restaurant, we sit, waiting to order. I want nothing to eat. All I know is a burning sensation in my vagina.

We stop by Mom's and Dad's on the way back to Birmingham. My sister Betty will later tell me what Dad says after Henry and I leave: "I don't think it happened for her. She doesn't look happy."

I HAD MET HENRY, a fraternity guy, my sophomore year of college in fall of 1965. He was a twin. The other twin died in his mother's womb. Katie, his mother, trained as a nurse, saved Henry from polio when he was ten years old by breaking his fever before the disease had time to travel through his body.

Carol, one of my sorority sisters, introduced us, and suddenly it seemed I was supposed to go out with Henry only. That was the way with college kids at the time. Young women were dating fraternity boys, getting pinned and were serenaded by the brothers below their dorm windows.

I tried to ignore Henry's personality—his nervous laugh that rang above everyone else's, the way he needed to brag about his fraternity, the Hayes family heritage.

The Hayes claimed that they had roots in Southern aristocracy, and to prove it they displayed the proper china—Carlton Blue, I think, and Reed & Barton silverware from their Virginia inheritance. All of them, his mother Katie, father Gil, and Katie's mother, lived in a cramped, gothic apartment heavily furnished with knickknacks. Henry lived there when he wasn't living in the dorm.

Every Sunday during our engagement, at about 1:00 p.m., Henry and I arrived after Anglican mass at St. Andrew's Church, the fragrance of holy incense clinging to our clothes. I could still hear the chant of the mass in my head. Like the mass, this weekly visit to Henry's family was an archaic and strange ritual. The apartment had dark walls, and the only light other than low wattage lamps was filtered sunshine through voile curtains. While we waited for lunch to be ready, we sat on the brocade love seat where Henry slept when he was home.

We ate the same lunch every Sunday—rare pork roast, asparagus, mashed potatoes, and dessert. Henry's father was always jovial after his lunchtime toddy, and his mother fussed over the table, brought out fine china, silverware, and linen of the "ancestry." Henry's laugh was nervous, too loud.

He wants to impress me.

At least he wants me. A marriage to him will be stable. That should be enough.

AFTER OUR JULY WEDDING, we moved into our love nest in campus student housing. I walked about the one-bedroom apartment like Eliot's Prufrock, measuring out my life in coffee spoons. I followed a daily ritual: by 10:00 a.m., I had planned the exact timing of dinner—*roast, potatoes, carrots, onions from the grocery, have the roast searing by 3:00 p.m., add cut vegetables by 4:00, cook until 6:00 p.m. exactly.* On Mondays, I wrote out the week's menu. I folded bath towels and placed them in even stacks in the linen closet— blue set in this stack, green in this one. I dusted the furniture. What else was there to do in this tiny, two-room apartment, except read *Beowulf* for English class and Voltaire's writings for French, or look out the bedroom window to see if the woman in the next apartment building had decided, again, to stand naked in her bedroom window?

Anything to break the monotony.

The rest of the day gathered around me like a warm blanket, thrown off on a steamy Southern afternoon. I stared at the wall and wondered if there was more to marriage than ritual and boredom? I had watched my sister Marge go through these motions. She seemed so happy, so content. Why wasn't I? Only years later would I realize I had created a bubble of perfection around her life, one that would burst all too easily.

Henry and I had infrequent sex, but when we did, I closed my eyes and moaned, pretending to be excited. Then he came easily, quickly, telling me that he liked the sounds I made.

I just wanted to get it over with.

The Leaving

12

FOR THE TWO YEARS AFTER Henry and I married in 1966, Dad settled into the quiet and slow rhythms of a wounded, aging animal, suffering one medical problem after another—bleeding ulcer, emphysema, and finally, an abdominal aneurysm.

Only after his death did we find that he had suffered an ulcer in New Guinea at the end of World War II. At the time, some twenty plus years earlier, my mother thought his bleeding ulcer must have had its origin in wartime stress. But ulcers can be traced to excessive drinking, acid imbalance, or bacterial infection. All are possible factors of military service in New Guinea, where bacteria was rampant, alcohol was plentiful, and soldiers were lonely, even scared.

His illnesses correspond to who he was.

His emphysema. My eyes burn as I remember riding in the back seat of our car for many years and on many trips over the blue highways of the United States. His smoke in my face. Rooms filled with smoke and television sounds, the crinkling of the empty pack of Lucky Strikes, Chesterfields, or Camels, the smell of lighter fluid and the intake of breath. His denial, his forgetting, when the doctor told him to stop smoking. This habit, like alcohol, was a highway dug and blasted through Dad's lungs, much like the roads, bridges, and airfields he built in the jungles of New Guinea.

An aneurysm would finally take him—a fatal bursting in the groin, a muffled cry. An apt metaphor for too much pressure from life's burdens, too much self-defeat, too little praise and encouragement. His despair burst, drowned out his manly power. Vessels broke open and sapped his life.

On March 10, 1968, Dad was transported via ambulance sixty-five miles from Hartselle to the Baptist Medical Center in Birmingham, Alabama. A young surgeon operated on his aneurysm as soon as he arrived.

THE NEXT DAY, I visited Dad in Intensive Care. Yesterday, I said, "I love you, Dad."

I think he nodded his head. I think he heard me.

On March 12, during winter term final exams, I received a telephone call from my cousin June, who was with Mom at the hospital. It was very late, near midnight, and it had rained most of the day. Henry and I drove quickly to the hospital and hurried to the Intensive Care waiting room where Mom and June sat quietly in the half-darkness. Shadows of hospital staff moved back and forth behind curtains in the Care Unit, and bleeping machines that track heart rate and blood pressure penetrated the quiet. I heard the soft squeaking of nurses' leather shoes on the polished floor.

The door to Intensive Care opened, and the young surgeon walked toward my mother.

"Your husband is gone. I'm so sorry. I couldn't save him."

Woodford Owen Nelson, dead at age 62.

The young doctor's voice caught as he tried to explain that he could not repair the damage done by the ruptured aneurysm.

It was still raining two hours later when Henry and I drove Mom over the slick interstate highway to Hartselle. No one spoke. In steady rhythm, heavy rain slapped the windows.

As we drove, I retrieved memories of my father. I knew I could choose to remember only his sense of failure, his addictions, or his pain of being the black sheep of the family when his parents wanted him to be a preacher, even his demotion later in his career from lieutenant colonel to master sergeant, a blow from which he never fully recovered. During my life with him, I was unable to separate his pain from my own.

I couldn't help him.

But instead, during that hour-long drive through the slashing rain, I thought of the times with him that held precious sweetness.

There was the day in May 1964, when as a senior in high school, I was told I would be valedictorian of my class.

At home, I waited for Dad's arrival from work. I heard his car drive into the carport, and I heard the side door open.

Mom told him, "Owen, Nancy has some news for you. She's in her room."

My mom's voice controlled her excitement.

He walked down the hall and entered through my open bedroom door.

"Dad, I'm Valedictorian of my graduating class!"

His face broke open in a lopsided smile. Valedictorian of my senior class in the very school he and his brothers and sisters, his mother, had attended.

I made him happy that day.

There is another day in May 1965, when he and Mom visited the campus of Birmingham-Southern College to witness my induction into the Mortar Board academic club. 'Southern was Dad's alma mater, where he worked in the post office, drank with his Kappa Alpha brothers, and played on the college baseball team.

This is surprise visit because I didn't know that I had earned this honor, awarded to students with at least a 3.0 grade point average. On that day, Dad held his shorter right arm against his chest. He stood erect like a soldier, now in his dark suit, a mere ghost of the young passionate man who lived and breathed the air of this very campus four decades ago. He smiled at me that day too, but as always, I found it hard to accept his joy at my achievement.

I always struggled to receive my father's approval when it finally came. I held it carefully so that I would not drop it, like a fragile glass egg. I could not embrace it fully for fear it would shatter.

BEFORE LEAVING BIRMINGHAM on that rainy night, we called my dad's sister Evelyn, and when we arrived at the house on Short Street, the lights were on throughout the house. Evelyn had removed Dad's slippers and his round glass ashtray from beside the stuffed chair where he sat to watch TV. No one said much. There wasn't much to say.

Rain continued through the day of the funeral, March 16, my parents' fortieth anniversary. The service was held in the blue and white sanctuary where Henry and I married less than two years before, where I held my dad's thin right arm as we moved down the aisle.

At that time, the Nelson plot at Hartselle Memory Gardens held the graves of Robert Goodwin Owen and Nancy Jane Owen, my great grandparents, Steve and Ellie Nelson, my grandparents, and their baby, Roberta Loreen. Dad was the first of Ellie's and Steve's children to be buried there.

MOM, BETTY, DWAYNE, HENRY AND I stand under the rain canopy by the freshly dug grave. Marge is not here. She is too ill and upset to come. An Army rifle squad shoots a nine-gun salute, three rounds. Their shots tear ragged holes in the grey air that hangs over the Hartselle Memorial Cemetery. We all startle, especially Betty, who jumps for all three rounds. In formation, the squad folds the flag that adorned Dad's coffin into a tight triangle. They present it to Mom.

"If Owen had lived, we would celebrate our fortieth anniversary on March 16," Mom will say through the next days and nights, as if talking to herself.

IN A PHOTO taken only months before his death, Dad stands on the front porch in his red plaid bathrobe and his dress hat, waving goodbye to me as I drive back to college. I had visited without Henry that weekend. During the night I jerked from sleep three, four, five times to hear the grating, cavernous coughing from his desiccated chest.

And still, I could not help him.

Seize the Day

13

JANUARY 1970. Less than two years after Dad's death, I was restless, annoyed with my domestic routine and uninterested in sex with my husband. I had an affair with a married man, my favorite college English professor, George. All it took was a conversation between us. Both of us were half-drunk.

"I love you, George."

"I love you too, Nancy."

All my life, I'd been the smart girl who obeyed all the rules. Yet I'd had feelings, ones I pushed aside to keep being "good."

At five years old, I felt a strange sensation in my groin when I stroked my teddy bear, Fido. At eight years old, I thought I was in love with my Sunday school teacher, an Army captain. I think I begged him to push me in the swing after church, and I deliberately kicked off one of my Mary Jane shoes so he would retrieve it and put it on my foot, like the prince Cinderella married. When I was nine years old, I wanted Daddy to pick me up and carry me around. I wondered why he was so distant, so unwilling to be near me. I didn't understand that he was being careful not to cross healthy boundaries with his youngest daughter. I felt sad, like maybe he didn't like me.

During my childhood, I wore the haircut Dad chose for me, a boyish style just below the ears. Both of my sisters wore their hair shoulder-length, and I loved to fantasize about having long hair.

During a church dance, a preacher in Sault Ste. Marie had told me my dad wanted a son and he got me. That comment stung, but I never said anything. I did wonder, however, if it was true.

During my teen years, I didn't feel pretty so it was easy to be "good." I was overweight, and my underdeveloped breasts, merely a 32 AA when I finally bought my first bra at age thirteen, were dwarfed above my thick waist. I allowed my high school steady boyfriend to kiss me, but that's all. Dad was careful to instruct me when I started seeing boys: "If a boy puts his hands where he's not supposed to, come home right away." He never really stated *where* the forbidden places were on my body. In fact, we didn't discuss sex at all. I guess he thought I'd know by instinct. I was so naive that I didn't even know my body. *Wasn't it sinful to know my body?* When I dated Henry, I was supposed to be a woman, and my first sign was that the roof of my mouth tingled when he caressed my nipples.

I knew nothing about sex, but I was tired of being a good, smart girl.

In January, a year and a half after Dad's death, I responded to George's gesture at a party. I wanted to know the secrets and lusting in a dark bedroom, the heart longings for an impossible love. I wanted to *seize the day*.

I was bored with Henry. Dad was gone. He wouldn't know.

Within two weeks of beginning the affair, I was ready to leave Henry. I called George one evening to tell him.

"I'm leaving Henry. I can't stay with him any longer."

On the other end of the phone, there was silence, then a few words from George.

"Ellen and I will be over in a few minutes."

At our dining room table, the four of us, George and his wife Ellen, Henry and I, talked as if we were discussing a current event or a vacation. There were no raised voices, no accusations of infidelity. Henry's face looked reddened and surprised, as if he'd been slapped. I could see he'd suspected nothing. He met my expectations. He did not fight for me. He did nothing but comply.

Ellen's lack of reaction surprised me. Later, I found out she'd experienced her husband's dalliances with other women.

Henry was working as a new lawyer in a firm downtown. We asked his boss, Mr. Princeton, to handle the divorce.

As soon as possible, I moved into an apartment, freshly painted with polished wood floors. The building itself, a 1930s structure, gave me a sense of stability. This was the first time I'd ever lived alone, without parental supervision, without a husband. In this apartment, I had autonomy. I was happy that I could do what I wanted in my own place, sparse as it was. I entertained friends from my church. I played and then played again Simon and Garfunkel's latest release "Bridge Over Troubled Water," feeling somehow the deep importance of friends.

GEORGE TOLD ME he would not leave his wife and family. But I was desperate to be with him. I'd openly defied my marriage vows. I'd cut myself off from any emotional support I had from Henry, my father had died, and my mother lived over sixty miles away in Hartselle. I was alone.

Then in early February, a test confirmed that my baby was due in October. The father could only be George, as I had not slept with Henry for over three months.

I was ecstatic. At least I would have someone else in my life. I'd have a part of George. And maybe he'd change his mind.

I was thin, 106 pounds, and gaunt. My clothes hung loose, and my hipbones protruded. It was as if my whole body was being channeled into this new life.

George was not pleased. He hinted that I should "take care of it," but I was resolute. I wanted this baby.

IN LATE FEBRUARY, I begin cramping and spotting. My pulse quickens as my clammy hands grasp the phone; I call my high school friend Pam, who lives nearby. "I'll be right over," she speaks quickly and hangs up the phone. She arrives in minutes, with towels and pads to catch the bleeding. I can barely walk to the door and unlock it to let her in.

I lie on my mattress as I weep and soak up the blood in towels.

I call my doctor, who tells me, "Catch the fetus in tissue and bring it into the office tomorrow." I'm guessing he wants to examine the tissue for diagnostic reasons, but there is no emotion in his voice, no caring or sorrow. *Catch "it?" My baby has become a thing, not a life. Something to be discarded in the waste can.*

The next day, I enter my doctor's office with a brown paper bag full of bloody tissue. After an examination, the doctor schedules a D and C for me at the local Catholic hospital. During my recovery, George brings me a book, *The Dark Night of the Soul.* He leaves after only a few minutes.

When I return to my apartment, I am alone. My shoes make clicking sounds, echoes on the newly waxed wooden floors.

I grieve for this child. I grieve for Dad, dead only two years. *How would he feel if he knew what I had done?*

BY THE END OF THE SUMMER, it was clear that George would not leave his wife. I was devastated. For days I continued my local library job, working robotically, then coming home to sleep. I woke up one morning in my apartment alone, with no prospects of any kind. I knew I had to give my life some direction. I decided to apply for graduate school. I had a good college record, with Phi Beta Kappa membership, so after submitting applications to four universities, I was offered a fellowship and two scholarships. I chose Auburn University's teaching fellowship, which allowed me to follow in my mother's footsteps. Auburn is in rural southeast Alabama. I would be near enough to visit my mother.

I saw George one more time shortly before I left Birmingham. He was drinking, and he promised to marry me. But the morning after, when I was at breakfast at my friend Helen's house, Ellen called. She had admitted him to the hospital psych ward. He had been drunk and calling my name. I heard later that he underwent electroshock therapy.

George and Ellen remained married until she was killed in a car accident, some fifteen years later. A mutual friend mailed the obituary to me.

I would not hear from George again until the 1990s, when I wrote him a letter after finding his address on the Internet. We exchanged infrequent letters as former student and former professor, until his death in 2013. And in them, he acknowledged his affairs as "frauds." He loved his wife until the end.

I GRAPPLED with my new role as graduate student, trying to forget the man I thought was my true love while hoping after all that I could be with him. I wanted a miracle.

One night in October, the month when my son (somehow I knew it would be a boy) would have been born, I awoke in my apartment with a poem in my head, a lament to my lost child.

> *This silence only magnifies the echo*
> *Of all my love, and fear, and shame,*
> *And of the little life which was to be*
> *on this our day.*

I jotted down these lines before I could forget them and went back to sleep.

A few nights later, my father came to me while in half-sleep. He stood next to my bed. He looked much like he had in later life—a balding head, khaki pants and shirt. But he stood tall, as if he was somehow renewed, healed from his war experiences, from his drinking and smoking. Healed in spirit.

He slowly turned and walked out of my room. I heard no footsteps. He seemed to be floating.

He was making sure I was safe. And at that moment, I was.

The Second Time Around

14

IF I WANTED EXCITEMENT, why didn't I stay with Bill? After all, he gave me my son. But our relationship proved to be explosive. We were two Geminis, but we were anything but twins. If we each had two sides, you could count on the negative face of one of us showing up when the positive side was showing itself to the other.

In summer 1975, five years after my divorce and miscarriage, I had earned my master's degree. I had suffered another disastrous affair with Jack, a math student and a former helicopter pilot in Vietnam, but fortunately did not marry. For the time, I was done with men and with grad school. I needed a break. I moved to Birmingham, where I had friends who could help me find work.

Then I met Bill at a storefront church service of a Baptist minister. The minister had left his city church because the congregation refused to integrate. This was the time of racial tension in the city that remained after the Selma march, the Sixteenth Street Baptist Church bombing, and Martin Luther King's assassination.

When I first glanced at Bill, I noticed the broad shoulders, burly arms, and body of a high school weightlifter and football player. He had a powerful, masculine frame. He had served a tour of duty on the *U.S.S. Kittyhawk* in the early 1970s. During his tour of duty, he'd witnessed the engine fire and race riot that took place on the ship.

That Sunday, and for the first weeks of our relationship, he seemed very mature, very much in control of himself. He had a mother, a brother and sister, all of whom were very welcoming when he brought me to meet them for the first time. I liked the feeling of family.

It wasn't long before Bill and I rented a second-floor apartment of a 1930s brick house in Birmingham's historic Southside community. I enjoyed its traditional architecture, the fireplace, the view of the city from the screened back porch. Lights twinkled in the valley that is Birmingham, and the torch of the statue Vulcan, icon of Birmingham's steel industry, shone high and proud in his right hand, his arm raised to the sky. When a city resident died in a car accident, Vulcan's torch was red against the dark night sky. Otherwise, it was green.

BECAUSE OF MY ONGOING NEED for stability, Bill and I ignored our clashing personalities. Even the minister who married us felt us unsuited. But as far as I was concerned, the die had been cast, a wedding planned, lives together begun. I assured myself that we would work out our differences with time and maturity.

We lived the first three years of our marriage in Auburn, Alabama, where I completed my dissertation and he, his bachelor's degree. In 1979, we moved to Michigan, where I had been hired at a small college as assistant professor to replace someone on sabbatical.

Moving away from Alabama, from the telling light of the Vulcan statue, did little to improve our marriage. On an average, the light was red more than it was green. But when it was green, it was a bright and rich color.

AFTER A YEAR of full-time teaching at Albion College, I decided I wanted a child. Our marriage had its problems, but I knew at age thirty-three that my time was limited. In January 1980, I became pregnant. I remember the quiet Sunday afternoon, snow falling gently outside. We only tried once.

My baby would be born in October, ten years to the month after the baby I lost. I wanted to sweeten my marriage to Bill with this child, to curb the anger and outbursts. I wanted to make our home more secure and healthy.

I should have known that I couldn't solve a marriage with a child. But at that time, on that day, the light was a rich, emerald green. And to me, green meant growth, new life, hope, moving forward.

IT'S ONLY WITH YEARS of reflection and healing that I have come to understand the meaning behind "a bad match." I was drawn to Bill for the positive side of his Gemini personality—warmth, gregariousness, love of reading and learning. But when our two selves clashed, the impact was volatile and hurtful.

Decades have passed, and we've both grown. Now Bill is a family friend to me and to my husband; he is a source of humor and warmth. We shared the loss of his sister, Mary, who remained my friend through years of estrangement. We shared the loss of my sister Betty. We talk about our son and the cultural differences in the places we live—he in the South and I in the Midwest. And we find more similarities between us, more times of deep conversation between two Geminis, who now reveal their best faces to one another.

Evan and Ted

15

MY MARRIAGE TO BILL ended in 1982, after I'd taken a tenure-track teaching job at a two-year college in the Detroit area. For the next few years, I would raise my son, teach classes and research the writings of Frederick Manfred, Minnesota writer. My life was full.

For the first time, I had another life under my care. I bought my first house alone and enrolled my son in a school for gifted children.

I had done it all by myself—divorced with a small baby, taken on a full-time job, moved to a city, bought a house. I was, for all intents and purposes, a strong woman. But I was lonely. Encouraged by friends, I entered a personal ad in the *Detroit Free Press* and met Evan, a kind man who would become my third husband.

WE MARRIED in the spring of 1984 at a good friend's house. My mother read aloud Shakespeare's Sonnet 116, "Let me not to the Marriage of True Minds Admit Impediment." Because of Evan's Scottish lineage, we hired a bagpiper to play briefly, and I walked down the stairs to a piano recording I had made of Satie's *Gymnopedie I*. According to the arrangement, it should be played "Lent et douloureux" (slow and mournfully). I did not know that day how this music would reflect the journey I was about to take.

Evan and I moved into a new, large house, a sprawling ranch house in a Detroit, Michigan suburb. The neighborhood has a distinctive architectural history. Henry Ford planned the streets in this small subdivision, and he constructed the nearby townhouses in the 1930s. The division was encircled by lovely sidewalks, gardens, and enclosed courtyards, forming the appearance of a close community, a concept I had not experienced.

Many of the families who lived nearby married and raised their children in this neighborhood for years, within the shadows of one another's doors. It was like a tribal village. All of the families knew one another. On a Sunday morning, one mother might cross the street in her nightgown, bathrobe, and slippers, to visit with her neighbor. The children slept back and forth among the houses and roamed the streets in groups, as if they had sprung from the same seed.

Soon I found that I couldn't breathe in this community. I could not shake that feeling of entrapment. I feared stasis.

Don't stay too long in one place. You might disappear. The message from my childhood. This thought haunted me as I attempted to settle into this new life.

My marriage fell into a predictable pattern. Evan was building his new business with a partner, and daily, he left early for work and dropped off my five-year-old son at his private school. I taught classes, came home to my basement study to grade papers, prepared for the next day's classes, wrote reviews and critical papers, and edited Frederick Manfred's letters for publication. I picked up Owen at school, Evan returned from work, and we had dinner. Afterward, Evan sipped scotch-on-the-rocks while he sat on the couch. He often fell asleep in front of the TV. I should have known this was normal, given his work schedule, but it frightened me. It was too much like my dad.

Same old, same old.

By the next spring, as the days and weeks passed in the fall, I found myself absorbed in the view outside the window of my basement study. I watched the green grass disappear beneath snow until I could barely see above the drifts. As the snow melted, it left brown, dead grass. By May, it returned to rich green.

I was bored. I craved excitement and change. I tried to reason with myself, to understand my relentless need for excitement. I needed someone, not a silent man in front of the TV. I wanted someone to talk with about everything under the sun.

At a Friday afternoon happy hour for the college English Department, I sat next to Ted, a seasoned faculty member and union leader. At the time, he was in his late fifties and the top of his head was balding, but his body was the lean frame of an athlete. He had been on my hiring committee, and I'd heard stories about the early years of the department, about the pick-up basketball games he played with his colleagues. I'd heard about the sharp jab of his elbow when he went for the basket.

What I noticed that day was his leg against mine, a gentle pressure that could almost be accidental. He pushed against me again, and again.

Somehow, Ted must have caught the primal scent of my restlessness.

The table was littered with empty beer bottles and ashes from the smoldering cigarette butts Ted pressed into the plastic ashtray. Bob Seeger's "Running against the Wind" played from a speaker, and the talk and laughter grew louder as the drinks were served. I looked around to see if anyone noticed. No one looked at us. Everyone drank beer or wine, talked and laughed.

I'd just been married a year, but I found myself responding. I pressed my leg against Ted's.

I could feel him staring at me for several minutes. Finally, I looked up at him. I couldn't seem to break the gaze. I searched his face, tanned and lined from the sun, his upper lip permanently arched from years of holding a cigarette. A person could think it was a sneer if he didn't know Ted's personality.

After that day, I noticed the slightest hint of springtime's turning to summer; I studied the roses blooming in our garden, every new bud, a flowering bush. I breathed in the scent of fresh-cut grass. After the encounter with Ted, my skin felt sensitive to touch.

I awakened.

ONE DAY several weeks after the happy hour, I hurried into the division office, where Ted and some other colleagues sat and smoked between classes. Those were the days when people smoked inside offices and classrooms. The men puffed and joked, punned and laughed about a student's English blunder. The room was small, and with Ted and I both there, it felt close.

Ted winked at me, and I could feel his eyes on me. He looked at my body, my legs underneath my short skirt, my hair in a curly perm, the way I walked.

I had seen him flirt at parties, but after that happy hour I was unable to act normal around him in front of others. I struggled to smile, and I left the office as quickly as I entered.

During my quick trip to check my mail, I pulled out a sealed envelope with no stamp, my name typed on the outside. I knew what to expect. I had received these notes for weeks. I knew it contained a poem written to me, either an original by Ted, or one by a famous poet who wrote erotic poetry.

Today's poem is William Carlos Williams' "This is Just to Say." Two days before, I had given Ted two fresh grapefruits from a box of fruit I bought at my son's school.

> *I have eaten*
> *the plums*
> *that were in*
> *the icebox*
>
> *and which*
> *you were probably*
> *saving*
> *for breakfast*

> *Forgive me*
> *they were delicious*
> *so sweet*
> *and so cold*

I knew this was about me, about my breasts as he stroked them in a wooded area along a seldom-traveled county park road. Forbidden fruit.

"Yield not to temptation, / for yielding is sin," says the old hymn.

We met often at various spots in the public park, off the road and under a blanket of trees. Once, a policeman drove up to Ted's car where we sat and talked. "I'd be careful about where you meet your boyfriend," he said to me through the passenger window. He ignored Ted.

We were like teenagers stealing away, hiding from our parents.

"Each victory will help you / One other to win," the hymn continues. *What would Dad think?*

My father's image hovered. With all of his struggles, he held to his faith and the morality of his religion. He expected me to be pure.

TED AND I passed each other daily in the division office or hallway. We tried to act as if nothing had happened between us. We met often for coffee, outside on a bench.

His wife Darlene was an adjunct in the department. I could tell Darlene became suspicious when Ted saved me a seat at the memorial service for one of the deans of the college. She had to find her own seat. I could feel her eyes from the back of the room. I pushed aside the idea of how she must feel. *Ted knows what he's doing. Maybe he's preparing to separate from her.*

Because Evan was in his own world, he didn't notice my distraction, my wanting to spend more time in my study, writing. He returned from work in early evening, so he didn't know about my afternoon trysts in the park before I picked up Owen from school.

IT WAS WEEKS NOW, since our flirtation began. Ted was impatient. We had only gone so far in our stolen moments in the park. So much of my life had been about longing for what I could not have, not wanting what I had. I worried about my marriage, about the hurt I would give to my husband, a gentle man. But the idea of an older man, a campus leader, excited me.

I thought about my two failed marriages. I thought about Evan, who loved Owen as his own son. I shuddered when I considered what Dad would think about my committing adultery. He expected me to be pure and Christian. Since he had died, much had happened—my affair with an English professor from college, my divorce from Henry, lovers, marriage and divorce from my second, Bill. He never knew he had a grandson named for him.

And now a third divorce loomed. Here I was again, about to jump off a cliff into a void.

In late May, I was scheduled to deliver the annual faculty lecture on my research and editing of the letters of author Frederick Manfred. I had begun the editing process three years earlier in Sioux Falls, South Dakota and would return that summer for a six-week institute.

The morning of the lecture, I copied the ending of James Joyce's *Ulysses* on a note card. In this passage, Molly Bloom affirms life and her sexuality: "… and then he asked me would I yes to say yes my mountain flower and first I put my arms around him yes and drew him down to me so he could feel my breasts all perfume yes and his heart was going like mad and yes I said yes I will yes." I left the note card in Ted's mailbox.

No turning back.

In late morning, I stood before a crowd of one hundred people in a lecture hall. My hands trembled. The atmosphere in the room was heavy, captured by walls of a dark orange, a two-decades-old 1960s color. I had forty-five minutes to speak, and, as usual, too much material—lecture notes, overheads, slides. In the midst of the lecture, some of the papers left my fingers and floated to the floor. I made some joke about having too much material anyway. I was calm and centered until I looked up to see Ted sit down next to Evan. He smiled at me. He must have read the note.

Why did he deliberately choose the seat next to my husband?

I forced my attention back to my notes and slides.

It was hard to concentrate. I felt my heart beating fiercely against my green suit jacket.

Can I get through this lecture with Ted sitting so close to Evan?

Later, when Evan and I were in negotiations about divorce, he told me that Ted's breath smelled of whiskey that morning.

IN EARLY AFTERNOON, after the lecture is over, Evan leaves for work. Ted and I drive to a motel on a main road near the college. Ted returns from the office with a room key. He's carrying a six-pack of beer.

Today I am dressed for my lecture in my business suit, stockings and heels. Ted wears his usual dress pants and a plaid, long-sleeve shirt, his sleeves rolled up to reveal his long hands and fingers, tanned deep brown from playing basketball outside and from polishing Petoskey stones. His favorite hobby allows him to polish millions-of-years-old fossilized animals until they show the outlines of tiny bodies, joined together.

I imagine those hands, those fingers, stroking my body.

I use the bathroom, and then undress, casting my jacket, skirt, shoes and stockings, a silk blouse, and finally my bra on a chair. We do not speak. This is a kind of sacrament. Talk would mar it.

Ted has undressed rapidly, so he can watch me as I go through the ritual. I try to see myself as he sees me, and his eyes reflect me as I move about the room. He's told me some about his visits to topless clubs at lunch or on an afternoon, drinking beer in the dark, smoky bar with loud music. Topless women serve him beer, and in my imagination, their large breasts hover over the tray of bottles and cans. This afternoon, I am suddenly self-conscious. Even on this warm May day, I am cold in my nakedness. My breasts were large and full only during my pregnancy and afterward, when I was nursing my baby. Since Owen was weaned several years ago, my breasts have returned to their firm smallness.

The afternoon light slips in around the tattered edges of the curtains. The motel is old, and the room has only a hard, double bed, worn cover, and pillows pressed flat by many years of use. I hear the cars rush by outside our window on the nearby road at 45 miles per hour. They sound very close.

We lie together. I smell booze and cigarettes on his skin. Ted's body is strong and lean.

I think of a leopard.

I do not think of sin.

The Road Calls
16

IN JUNE, after Owen goes to his dad's in Alabama, I head for Sioux Falls, South Dakota for my six weeks of research and teaching, my station wagon loaded with typewriter, radio/cassette player, books, and clothes. I drive alone for two days through western Michigan, past Chicago, and into Wisconsin and Minnesota, singing out loud with my tapes—love songs by the Commodores, "Once, Twice, Three Times a Lady," or Elton John's "Yellow Brick Road." I sing while the landscape west of Chicago becomes the green, lush farmlands of Wisconsin, and finally the rolling plains near the Mississippi River. I'm on the move again. On the way to change, to new adventure. It's not the blue highways of my childhood days, but I'm excited by motion and change.

I'm well-versed in travel.

ALMOST EVERY SUMMER during the 1950s, our family would drive two or three days on two-lane highways from wherever we were living at the time—Oklahoma, Texas, Indiana, Kentucky, Michigan, Missouri. Sometimes we'd be moving to a new military base, and sometimes we'd be headed for Morgan County in North Alabama, to visit my grandparents, Papa and Mama Steve Nelson, and Big Mama Chandler.

The trip always seems endless as I sit for hours in the back seat watching farmland and small towns and gas stations pass by. Below my shorts, my bare, moist legs stick to the plastic seat covers. We drive the truck routes through large cities, hit the rush-hour traffic and suffer in the oven of the still car, sweating and panting, breathing diesel fumes from the big truck in front of us. My tongue is parched. I watch for a gas station, maybe the red Texaco star, or the orange Gulf sign that looks like a lollypop. The Gulf sign reminds me of an Orange Crush. I want one, or a Dr. Pepper in a tall, cold 10-2-4 glass bottle. When we finally stop for gas, I drink a soda down in two gulps.

We always leave early in the morning, following Dad's edict that we get on the road so we can cover our five hundred-mile daily allotment. We are awake by 4:30, and Dad packs the car by 6:00, acting like the engineer to figure the best angle for each piece of luggage. Before Dad even starts the car, I am queasy, anticipating carsickness in the swaying back seat. In fact, I plan on it. Sometimes the taste of orange hard candy reminds me of the nausea, somehow associated with a Gulf Oil sign. Then I don't want an Orange Crush.

Mom and I (and my sister Marge, before she left home) play the alphabet game on the highway—who will be the first to find an "a" or a "b" or a "c" on a license plate or on a road sign? Over and over, I see the advertisements for Burma Shave, small rhyming signs spaced carefully so passengers in the cars could read them one by one as they pass at 50 miles per hour.

The wolf
Is shaved
So neat and trim
Red Riding Hood
Is chasing him.
BURMA-SHAVE

When I don't feel car sick, I think about an ice cream cone and ask Daddy to find a Dairy Queen. Most often he teases me, reaching out of the window as we drive through isolated farmland. He brings back a phantom cone, passing it to me in the back seat.

On our first day of the usual two-day trip, I wait and hope and ask for a motel with a swimming pool so I can cool off and maybe meet some other kids who, like me, are traveling American roads. I wonder if they travel as much as we do.

If we are moving to a new base, I think about what our new home will be like. If we're going home to Alabama, I think about my grandparents, the scent of moist southern air in the evening, fresh biscuits and dogwood, lightning bugs and squeaking screens.

American motion, restlessness. Our lives were like that. Always going somewhere.

AFTER TWO DAYS on the road to Sioux Falls, I arrived in late evening. I was prepared to teach in a summer Mellon Institute and work for six weeks on the publication of the Manfred letters. I loaded my luggage, typewriter, and my radio into the dormitory room with its brick walls, concrete floor, and a single air-conditioning unit below the window. Very spartan. A great place for me to work and think.

But I missed Ted.

I thought of him throughout the drive while I composed poems about travel and movement. In the motel, I wrote a poem, a parody of the John Donne's "A Valediction, Forbidding Mourning." Ted and I are "as stiffe twin compasses are two / [His] soule the fixt foot, makes no show / To move, but doth, if the'other doe."

THE DIRECTOR of the Mellon Institute was a friend, Art, who offered me the opportunity to teach at the institute that summer. There was time also for research and writing. I anticipated seeing friends from summers before, two office managers, Marilyn and Jenna.

Classes began the next morning. Every day I taught a Western Literature class, and my students and I attended a composition class and a lecture on western history. The turmoil of my life in Michigan seemed far away.

TWO EVENINGS LATER, Ted calls me in my dorm room. I'm deep inside Willa Cather's novel *My Ántonia,* concentrating on Jim Burden's journey back home to reclaim his connection to the land. The ringing of the phone bounces off the walls, and I jump. Ted is calling from a phone booth in a bowling alley near his house. I can hear the music and the banging of bowling balls, solid and echoing, on the lanes.

"Nancy, I've got to talk with you. I'm at Charley's Bowling Alley. I left the house because last night, Darlene found some of your love letters and poetry. She confronted me, and we argued. I told her I want a divorce. She knows I've not been happy. She won't admit that she hasn't been either. We haven't slept in the same bed for over ten years."

"Will you marry me?"

"Yes, I will."

I speak the words without hesitating, as if I've stepped from a high precipice into space, with no ground beneath me. The day of my lecture, when I drove with Ted to the shabby motel room, I knew we were risking everything—our marriages, our reputations, maybe even our jobs. I made my choice the morning I pulled my graduate school copy of *Ulysses* from the bookshelf and wrote Molly Bloom's words onto a small index card. Her "yes" was my "yes."

Sitting now on the creaky bed in the dormitory room, surrounded by concrete walls, I sense a familiar excitement, the adventure of the road always opening in front of me.

I love a challenge, a man I have to work for. Like the Army, always something exciting happening.

Two days later, I receive another call from Ted.

"Nancy, I was just admitted to the hospital with congestive heart failure."

Leaving Number Three

17

TED'S DAUGHTER had married that summer, and a few days before her wedding, Ted visited a doctor when he had difficulty breathing. The doctors told him to stop smoking and they gave him Coumadin, which would thin his blood and prevent another attack of congestive heart failure.

I was nine hundred miles away when he called. I was frantic. For the next six weeks in June and July, I wrote poems and mailed letters to Ted daily, sending them in care of a female colleague's mailbox. She took them to Ted in the hospital. She told me later that when she walked into his room, he was in bed on top of the covers, in pajamas and tennis shoes. I could imagine him with his long limbs, elbows and knees bent, lounging on the bed. When she handed him my letters, he clutched them close to his chest, as if they could heal his struggling heart.

After his release from the hospital a few days later, Ted told me, in letters and during phone calls, about the new apartment he planned to rent in Inkster, a nearby suburb. He told me he planned to talk to Darlene about a divorce.

I hadn't talked to Evan yet.

This is my chance to help a man save himself from a lifetime of destructive habits.

In late July, I left Sioux Falls to return to Michigan. This time, my mind was on the road, not on scenery or songs. So much had changed since I came west weeks before. So much to think about.

WE PLAN TO MEET in the afternoon of the second day of my trip home. I park at a motel parking lot near the airport and enter the lobby. My stomach knots up.

I'm a bad person, someone not to be trusted. Worst of all, I am a slut. And soon everyone will know it.

What would Dad think?

Ted opens the motel room door. His face is flushed, and he's lost weight. He has a fresh haircut that comes just above his ears. In some ways, he looks younger, like a new man. I can tell he's spent time outside; his tan is even deeper than when I left in June. Behind him on the small motel room table sits an ice bucket, a bottle of champagne, and a small gift-wrapped package. After we make love, I will open it to find a pair of diamond earrings.

Finally, I can touch him, the bristly beard he's grown because he knows I like it, his lean frame, sinewy and strong. Against my chest, I can feel his enlarged heart beating hard and steady.

The air conditioning grinds away, just loud enough to cover our sounds.

IN EARLY EVENING, I arrive home. I pull into the driveway, and Evan comes out to meet me. His face tells me he's relieved that I'm home.

Owen is visiting his father in Alabama, so the house is empty of his toy sounds—bells on a fire truck, the pinging of a plastic hammer against a plastic workbench.

It's just the two of us.

101

We eat a simple dinner of grilled cheese sandwiches, and then we drink Manhattans to celebrate my return. I say little about my trip or my six-week research and teaching experience. Instead, I sit away from Evan on the other end of the old brown plaid couch, watching TV.

I go to bed early, claiming fatigue.

The next morning, I wake up nauseous. I vomit until there is nothing left in my stomach and then gag more. After a blood test at the doctor's office, I'm told I have Salmonella. Something eaten during my road trip. I'm to eat only bread and water for ten days. My sickness gives me something to focus on until I'm able to tell Evan the truth.

Two days later, my nausea eases, but I let more days pass as I avoid the inevitable confrontation. I meet Ted for breakfast in the Red Wagon Restaurant. Above the clatter of dishes and silverware, the chatter of customers as the waitresses take orders, and the cook yelling out an order number, we talk about the future and the probable reaction of the other English teachers in our department.

"My buddies will laugh when they find out that we're together. I've always told them I like slim women, women with small breasts," he says, chuckling.

I think again of Ted's frequent visits to topless bars. I've never been inside one of them and wonder what they are like, whether any of the women have small breasts like mine. I'm sure they don't.

Of course, these male buddies will laugh with Ted, but only in private, not openly in the very public, small community of our college. They will wear a mask of shock, maybe even disdain, because Ted is committing adultery and leaving his wife of thirty years.

AS I THINK now about the weight of our decisions to leave our marriages, I realize that I did not think about the impact of our actions on our two families or on the people around us. I could not foresee that the situation would become dire, even life-threatening.

All I knew was that I had to go forward.

THE DAY CAME to tell Evan. For hours, I thought about our short marriage, his hard work with Owen, the plays and opera, fine dinners, his exquisite taste in clothing and furniture.

I thought of his respectful treatment of me, his patience with my son.

WHEN EVAN WALKS IN THE DOOR tonight, I waste no time. "I need to tell you that I'm having an affair with my colleague, Ted. I want a divorce. I'm sorry." He stands still in our kitchen, only months ago filled with the new pans and dishes of a hopeful marriage. He's a gentle man, but tonight he screams at me. This is a side of him I've never experienced.

Evan shouts as he pulls beers from the refrigerator and lugs them to our basement room. He drinks one beer after another, I don't know how many. A raw, primal scream emerges from downstairs, a glass bottle crashes against the fireplace. I take a deep breath to calm myself.

When I hear his uneven, angry footsteps as he climbs the stairs to the kitchen, I brace myself.

"The first time we went out, I thought you dressed like a dowdy old woman."

He's lashing out. His words hurt.

Now I understand why he bought me some strange-looking contemporary dresses, as if he wanted me to look like I stepped out of a New York magazine. He's never said a word about my style.

Why did he marry me if he thought I looked "dowdy"?

As he continues his rant, I feel anger rise in my throat.

"Fuck off! Get away from me!" I scream, and then I throw a trashcan at him, full of tin cans and greasy paper towels. The mess covers the tiled kitchen floor.

I escape for the night to a friend's house, where Evan and I were married only a year and a half ago.

The next morning, I go back to our house to pack my suitcase for the two-day trip. I will drive to Franklin, Kentucky, to pick up my son.

Evan is waiting for me. He's skipped work. His eyes are swollen from too much drink and from weeping.

He speaks first. "I'm sorry. I was angry and hurt when I said those things. I didn't mean it, what I said about the first time I saw you."

We talk quietly for a while about our divorce. He agrees to contact a lawyer so we can divide our possessions fairly and not have the expense of two lawyers. I realize this will be my third divorce, and all of them were handled by one lawyer. I've never had a fight in court.

When I leave, we hug gently. I'm saddened at my betrayal of a friend, a good man.

But I've already come too far to turn back.

BY MID-AUGUST, Ted moved into the apartment in Inkster, set back from the road on a wooded lot. In September, he filed for divorce. Evan had moved out of our ranch house on the hill in July, and I remained until we could sell it.

My third divorce was pending.

Divine Aphasia Images
(in chronological order)

First Christmas, December 1946

Nancy, Dad, Mom in Alaska ca 1952

Nelson leads his battalion, Alaska 1951-2

Dear Daddy,

How have you been lately and how is Taffy? I had a long holiday. Got off Thursday & Friday so with the weekend I had a pretty long holiday.

I think this last six weeks has been about the hardest in my life. I would come home, change clothes, & eat a snack. Then I would work sometimes intil 10:30 stopping only to eat supper. I was tired all the time.

My work paid off, though. I got a 94 in my Science 6 Weeks Test, a 98 in my Social Studies Six Weeks test and a 85 in my English 6 Weeks Test. I sure was happy. I don't know about my Math 6 Weeks Test yet. We get our Report Cards next week.

I am in my school news-

Letter from Nancy to Dad (1958) page 1

paper this time. I will explain about it to you. Even though I wasn't here our class had the most subscriptions for the paper so we got our picture in it. Some of us wrote to the paper things about ourselves. I wrote in and told them how I came here on the bus from Michigan. ~~That is tol~~ They make funny things up about what we write. That is why they said that about me.

I have to go now.

Love Always
Nancy

Letter from Nancy to Dad (1958) page 2

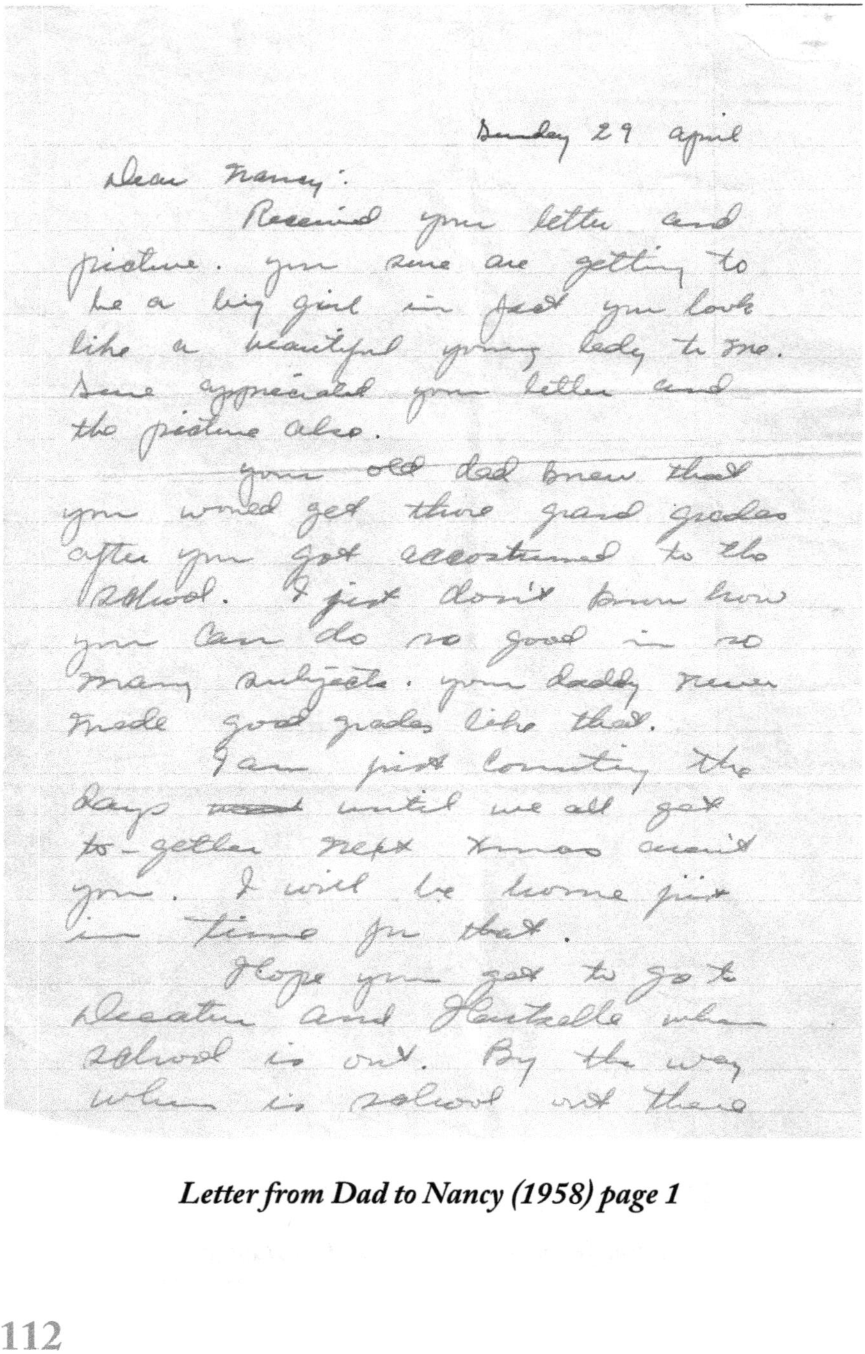

Sunday 29 April

Dear Nancy:

Received your letter and picture. You sure are getting to be a big girl in fact you look like a beautiful young lady to me. Sure appreciated your letter and the picture also.

Your old Dad knew that you would get those grand grades after you got accostumed to the school. I just don't know how you can do so good in so many subjects. Your daddy never made good grades like that.

I am just counting the days ~~until~~ until we all get to-gether next Xmas aren't you. I will be home just in time for that.

Hope you get to go to Decatur and Hartselle when school is out. By the way when is school out there

Letter from Dad to Nancy (1958) page 1

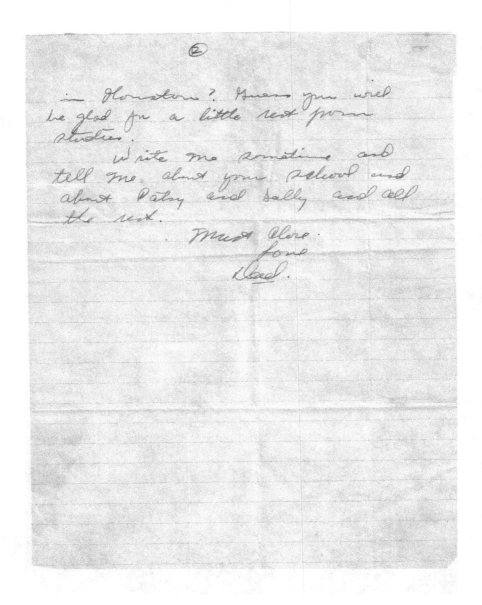

Letter from Dad to Nancy (1958) page 2

Nancy, 6th grade

First Wedding, 1966—Dad, Mom, Nancy, Marge, Betty

Graduation from Birmingham-Southern College, 1968

PhD, Auburn University, 1979

Visit to Sioux Ste. Marie, ca 1990

Reflections on Marriage

18

MY ROLE MODEL for marriage was my sister, Marge, and hers was a dream of the American family: husband, children, house, and permanence.

I watched her life, wanted to emulate her. She scheduled her time for the children, Rob Jr. and Terry, and the housekeeping, and she waited for Rob to come home each day. On a typical late afternoon, he would enter the front door calling out "Hi, Sweetie." Marge would have dinner cooking, the table set. She would hurry to meet him, and they would kiss, not just a peck, but a deep one. Regardless of who was visiting, in early evening they would retreat to the bedroom and close the door. Marge's obedience was a symbol of the notion of traditional marriage. Her kitchen cabinets were orderly, from the rows of juice glasses decorated with a pattern of oranges, to the small basket in which she kept her Double Mint chewing gum.

Her domestic paradise was short-lived.

In her early thirties, Marge was diagnosed with multiple sclerosis. I have no way of knowing whether other problems she had experienced—her nervous breakdown and the shock therapy, the uncertainties of constant change, Dad's drinking—all made her vulnerable to this condition. Even today, scientists still debate the

121

exact origins of MS. To me, her MS represented her protest against the limitations the world had placed on her.

The inflamed myelin sheath and the deterioration of Marge's nerve endings eroded her nervous system as well as her life and marriage. She had been a tall, attractive brunette, athletic in her childhood and teen years, but in later years after her diagnosis, her looks and vitality slowly evaporated.

By the time Robbie and Terry were teenagers it was evident that Marge's marriage, like her nervous system, was victim of a crossfire of confused and chaotic messages. Marge's beauty had remained with her in the first fifteen years of her disease, but then she became bloated and overweight, sallow-skinned. She lost power over her body.

By 1980, her marriage was over.

Mom reported that during one of Marge's visits home to Hartselle, the phone rang, and Mom answered. Rob asked to speak to Marge. There was no chitchat.

"I'm moving out. I'll be gone by the time you get home," he told her.

Marge gasped and sat down, then hung up the phone.

"He's leaving me. Rob is leaving me."

The couple had few assets; and when their divorce was final, Marge was left with only a small sum of money for support.

Betty, who lived nearby, kept us informed about our sister's decline. Rob was gone and the kids had moved out. Marge would prepare a meal, automatically repeating her wifely role. Betty told me that one evening, she cooked a large pot of spaghetti and meat sauce and ate one helping while she gazed out into the back yard where their two small children had played, and where their dog Woody had run back and forth chasing a ball.

After she finished eating, she walked to the stove, picked up the pot of sauce, then noodles, and threw the rest of the food into the sink. The meat and pasta disappeared into the garbage disposal.

Marge died in January 1996, after fifteen years of assisted living and nursing homes near Betty and her second husband John.

ALL OF MY MARRIAGES were my desperate efforts to fill the hole I had in my life, even while Dad was alive.

In my first marriage to Henry, I had just turned twenty years old and was still in college. Henry was a frat guy, and I wanted to get out of the dorm, so I married him.

Bill, my second, was the image of a strong male, a kind of "good seed" who would give me a baby. At the time, I was hooked on the idea of him, his warm and loving family, and I looked away from evidence of how mismatched we were.

My third husband, Evan, was gentleness itself, an artist who became a father to Owen when he was three years old, when my son already had many reasons to be angry. Evan worked with Owen's anger, nurtured his creativity. Even today as an adult, Owen has a strong relationship with Evan and his wife. For me, Evan was too calm, too gentle, too sweet. Obviously, I needed more challenge.

And then there was Ted, the epitome of my search. He was intelligent, shared my interests in literature and writing. He fit the model of the older man, the father, someone whose personality challenged me. And drinking and smoking were integral to his life. These habits were all too familiar.

Betrayal

19

FALL SEMESTER, 1985, commenced as usual, with meetings, class preparations and schedule shuffling. The college was just like a small village, and gossip traveled fast. News of my affair with Ted spread over the campus.

One morning as I walked into the small English Department office, I heard laughter from colleagues, several of Ted's long-time friends—two Edwards and a Colin—waiting for class. Ted was not there. The men had been exchanging their usual word jokes and puns, stories about their new students. As I opened the door, they suddenly stopped talking. The ends of their words hung in the air. The quiet was heavy.

Before the news got out, I would have joined in the banter, the discussions of humorous student papers or college politics. Now, I took a glance at my empty mailbox and quickly walked through the door into the hallway. I felt like Hester Prynne, the protagonist of *The Scarlet Letter*. I wore the badge of the "other woman," the initiator of a destructive affair, a scarlet "A" on my shoulder. In the long run, it wouldn't matter about Ted's participation, that he had approached me first. I'd already been tried and convicted.

That guilt was to visit me often during the whole of our relationship.

AS TED AND I SIT in his office later one afternoon, he lights a cigarette on the end of the last one and jiggles one foot on the floor, crossing and uncrossing his legs. Every few minutes, he clears his throat, even though he isn't hoarse. It was a habit I've noticed lately.

He must be tense about something.

I watch him more closely.

After a few minutes of idle talk, Ted tells me that a female colleague, Marsha, called him into her office. She was in tears about his separation and our relationship. She told him, supposedly in confidence, "Don't marry Nancy. She doesn't stay married long."

She doesn't stay married long. Echoes of my greatest fear, that I have no capacity to stay with anyone. My marriages have been short— Henry for three years, Bill for five, Evan for less than two years. But this relationship is different. Ted is the epitome of my longing for my father. An older man with problems, but someone who wants me. And someone who won't make it too easy. Easy is boring.

This one will work.

LATER, alone in Ted's apartment, we talk about the incident again. By now, I'm angry. "Why did you tell me about Marsha's comment? She asked that you keep her confidence."

He says nothing.

I persist. *By God, I'm going to discuss this intrusion!*

After he's quiet for a minute, I speak again.

"I want to confront her. I want to tell her I know what she said, and I want to say something to wound her. Most of all, I want to tell her to stay the fuck out of other people's business."

Ted face reddens, covering his tan.

He finally speaks.

"She talked to me in confidence! She'll know I told you!"

"Then why did you tell me? And why didn't you stand up for me?"

He's silent again.

In the coming days, I refuse to speak to Marsha, though I'm always careful to look her in the eye when I pass her. One day I enter the department office where she happens to be sitting alone. I sit down quietly near her, and I look in her direction until she leaves the room. *If Ted doesn't want me to talk to her, I won't. But I'll let her know how I feel, nonetheless.*

I FELT BETRAYED by Ted's refusal to defend me. At that time, I couldn't see why anyone would not understand our relationship. I was too caught up in the excitement and, after all, I told myself, we loved each other. He'd made his own choices. I remembered my father's disappointments in his Army career, his demotion. How he wanted to be respected and trusted by his peers, and how the military bureaucracy let him down. I wanted to believe that I was respected and trusted in my work life and my personal life.

I brushed aside any thoughts of Ted's family, the pain they might feel over all of this.

Divine Aphasia

20

JANUARY 6, 1986. This is the day when, according to legend, the three wise men arrived at the manger of Baby Jesus. For many Christians it is a time of prayer and reflection, of revelation.

We've just left an Epiphany party. Most of the evening, Ted sat near the booze and drank while I socialized. At the end of the evening, as we go for the car, he screams at me.

"I can't be what you want!" he yells over and over into the cold night air.

The other guests stop and watch as he curses and almost falls on the ice. I get in my car, start the engine, and drive away from him. I don't want to be near him. Like Dad, Ted turns into another person when he's loaded, loud instead of Dad's quiet, verbal instead of silent like Dad, who closed himself in a protective shell, staring into space.

Ted runs after my car. I finally stop and wait for him to get in. He's embarrassed me in front of our colleagues, but I can't leave him here without a ride home. I drive carefully from Farmington, Michigan, down the ice-lined Southfield Freeway that borders Detroit, to Ford Road. I turn west and head toward his apartment in Inkster.

"I can't be what you want. I can't meet your expectations," he mumbles as we ride along the icy highway, his whiskey breath misting the inside of the windshield.

"What expectations?"

"You want me to be all of these things for you—go to parties all the time. I don't like it."

"I don't know what you are talking about. Where did this come from? You said you wanted to go!"

As I drive, I ask myself other questions. *Why do I even try to reason with him? Why do I feel guilt and failure like I did when I tried to understand my dad?*

With Ted, I am always off balance, always wondering and uncertain about what will happen next. *Why do I seek out this punishment?* I'm hurting, but the feeling is familiar, somehow comforting, almost erotic.

Daddy is angry. But at least he's paying attention to me.

I rationalize about why I am in this situation. Ted's congestive heart condition actually made the situation more attractive. *Wasn't he in an unhappy marriage? Didn't the stress of his wife's confronting him when she found the letters from me, coupled with his daughter's marriage, cause the collapse of the heart?*

There was no epiphany on that night of questions. If I had revelations, I ignored them. As usual after arguments, we made up and went on as if nothing had happened.

DURING LATE JANUARY, I was spending a good deal of time in Ted's apartment. With the winter cold pressing against the windows, Ted smoked and watched television, sometimes read poetry. At night, he drank beer. He began with one or two, then increased his intake to four or five a night.

"Before I got sick, I drank fourteen beers a day," he boasted when I mentioned drinking and the effect on his heart.

"Four or five still seems too much to me. Remember what the doctor said." I tried to keep my voice from sounding shrill.

He didn't respond.

Dad pretended he didn't remember the doctor's warning about emphysema. He kept smoking anyway.

WHEN THE SEMESTER BEGINS the last week of January, Ted complains of an aching chest. We attend the birthday party of a colleague, and then return to Ted's apartment. That night he wears his usual jeans and a sweatshirt, tennis shoes and socks. I notice his gauntness. His collarbone stands out over the top of his shirt, and his jeans are loose. His face is sallower than tanned, and darkness under his eyes makes them seem to sink into his face.

Sitting in his living room, he talks about what he will leave his children when he dies. Suddenly, I'm the one who has trouble breathing. I begin to cry as I move over to be near him. I sit on the floor in front of his chair and put my hands and head on his lap. While I cry, he talks about his legacy and his children. He seems detached from me, as if I'm not even in the room. He pulls away from me, as if he's impatient with my sadness.

The next morning, a Saturday, I'm sleeping soundly at my ranch style house when I'm awakened around 7:30 a.m. by the phone ringing near my head.

"I need to go to the hospital," Ted's voice shakes. "I'll bring my car over to your house. You can drive."

I phone a neighbor friend and ask if I may drop off Owen to stay with her today. Back home, I shower and dress quickly. The doorbell rings. Ted is standing on my porch. Underneath his knit cap, Ted's face is bleached of color, more sallow than the night before.

We leave his brown, rusting Escort in my driveway and I drive my Subaru downtown to Henry Ford Hospital. On this grey winter morning, I move swiftly around cars on I-94 to Lodge Freeway, passing on the left and right. The roads are framed with gritty, grey snow and ice, nothing like the beauty of a fresh snowfall.

"Ted, are you okay?"

I glance quickly at him in the passenger seat. He stares at the bleak neighborhoods of low-income houses as we pass through West Detroit. He doesn't speak, doesn't even nod.

129

In the emergency room at Henry Ford Hospital, the nurse looks up his record, checks his pulse, and arranges for immediate admission.

Soon a young cardiologist looks at his chart, and he then listens to his heart and lungs with a stethoscope.

"Mr.__, you're having another episode of congestive heart failure. You've got fluid around your heart and in your lungs. Your heart isn't working at full capacity."

"Is he a candidate for a heart transplant?" I ask the question without knowing if Ted would want one.

The doctor doesn't hesitate a second to consider my question.

"No transplants for a patient with his habits."

He turns to Ted.

"You need to give up smoking and drinking."

After the doctor leaves the room, we sit for a long minute. Ted breaks the silence.

"I guess I'll have to give up one of my habits."

ON THAT SATURDAY, I began to keep what I called a "journal of love and growth." I reflected on Ted's recent illness, my fear that he might have pneumonia, that he might even die. I was determined to stick by Ted, to help him get better.

I couldn't help Dad, but maybe I can help Ted.

I wrote, "*Our lives are precarious. The doctor said his heart is functioning at a 15% capacity. It's his to decide if lifestyle changes (sans booze and cigs) will allow his heart to heal. Life is tenuous and I am happy in my decision to be with him. I feel a strength I haven't felt lately.*"

I know now that I was putting the best face on Ted's illness, hoping that it would somehow bring us together permanently.

I am at a perfect point in my life for productive growth. Forty years old, a son about to flourish, a lover, the best in my life. God, let me learn here, and grow!

The next day, Sunday, we speak on the phone. Ted tells me of visits from his two sons and his wife, Darlene.

"Stay home and catch up on your work. Call me tomorrow morning. I should be discharged by mid-morning and you can pick me up."

MONDAY MORNING, around 10:00 a.m., I call Ted's hospital room from my office phone. I expect to pick him up after my last class, around noon. I think I've dialed the wrong number. I don't recognize the voice on the other end of the phone.

"Nan, Nan, help, help … help me, Nan!" he repeats over and over. It's Ted alright, but something terrible has happened to him. I cancel my class and drive east on I-94 at 70 mph, taking a swift left into the Lodge Freeway and an illegal right exit onto a major boulevard to reach the hospital.

Let a cop try to stop me now.

I park my car in the hospital lot and rush to the cardiology floor. The hallway smells of rubbing alcohol and urine. Two men walk slowly up and down in hospital gowns and slippers, pulling IV poles, their catheters hung from them. In his room, Ted's bed lies empty, the sheets rumpled as if he's been struggling. A doctor I don't know enters.

"Your friend has suffered a stroke to the left side of the brain. His speech and reception are affected. He has aphasia. This means that he can't understand speech or speak clearly. He may never fully recover."

Never fully recover.

Attendants push Ted into the room on a rolling bed. He sits up in his hospital gown. The tie on the back of the gown has come undone, and it's open, making him seem helpless and vulnerable, like an unclothed child. When he sees me, he raises his long arms in the air and reaches toward me.

"Nan, Nan, where did it go? One, two, three, four, five, six, seven." He hits the flat of his hand on the top of his balding head.

After the orderly transfers him to his bed, I sit and hold his hand, making soothing sounds in my throat. As he struggles to speak, I think of Lucky's nonsense talk in Beckett's *Waiting for Godot*.

> "... *a world without meaning, without sense, without hope...from the heights of divine apathia divine athambia* **divine aphasia** ... *that man in short wastes and pines.*"

Now I understand why this play transformed me, shaped my understanding of life's meaning, or rather, its meaninglessness. Somehow, I have been preparing for this moment. And now I understand the meaning of aphasia. Ted sits on a dangerous precipice, his life precariously balanced. Mortality, the end of life, hovers over him: "...alas abandoned unfinished."

I have taught Becket's play for years, but I never imagined that I would see such futility firsthand.

The phone next to Ted's bed rings and I answer. It is Darlene. She asks to speak to Ted. "Ted has had a stroke. He has damage of the left brain, and can't hear or speak clearly." I hear her gasp on the other end of the phone.

This wasn't the way I'd imagined things going.

My journal that night:

> *I'm scared and alone, like a child in the dark.*
> *I want warmth, and light.*
> *Let me learn here, and grow.*

Stay with Your Mission
21

LIKE THE SOLDIER I had learned to be as a child, I was determined to stay with Ted, even after his stroke. I was jealous when the hospital staff deferred to Darlene for care decisions. She assumed her legal role as Ted's wife.

I noted in my journal Ted's struggles with language.

> *February 9. "Can you help me migweek?" is a question he keeps asking me. I don't know what he means. He kisses my right hand, small pecks one after another that seem desperate. God help us!*
>
> *February 10. Today he said "I want to help, but can't … I want to give you … I want to build something for you." The last part he articulated clearly. There is hope! I see my role as support. I want Ted to know I am here for him, regardless.*

The days after the stroke become surreal. Ted has many visitors, teachers from the college, friends, his children, his wife, and me. I time my visits so I don't run into Darlene.

One day, a nurse's aide speaks what she's been thinking.

133

"This is like a circus. I don't know which one of you he belongs to."

She diverts her eyes as she speaks to me, and I hear the judgment in her voice.

At the college, when I walk into the English Department office, instead of silence, I encounter questions about Ted's condition. Otherwise, nobody says much. It's not the time for banter.

The next Saturday is Valentine's Day. I visit Ted in the early evening, bringing chocolates and a huge card with hearts on it. I make sure I wait until everyone has had a chance to visit. Ted sits alone in his hospital gown, IVs in both arms. As we talk, we work together with paper and pen. I want to help him find the words he's lost, words from kindergarten—"cat," "hat," "boy," "sad." Soon he tires and we stop.

"Find another lover. Get a big man. Find a he-man for you, someone tough," he tells me.

These are the first complete sentences I've heard him speak in the six days since the stroke.

I say the words without pause. "If you want me, I will be here. I will *not* leave."

I DID CARE FOR TED and wanted to be with him. Perhaps I thought I'd gone too far along this road to turn back. Was I worried about public disapproval if I abandoned him now? Perhaps it was stubbornness, an unwillingness to say I'd made a mistake. Too many chess pieces had been moved on the board. There was no way to undo the moves.

I wanted Ted, the tough man, my answer to finding Dad. I wanted protection and stability. Now *I* was the one who had to be strong.

The day of discharge approached, and the doctors said Ted could not live alone, at least not for a while. Both Darlene and I spoke with the social worker, each of us pleading her case.

On the afternoon of discharge, Ted, Darlene, the social worker, and I gather in her office. The social worker repeats that someone must be with Ted around the clock, at least for the time being. She brings paper and markers so we can communicate with Ted. The room is stifling. I feel adrenaline pump through my body. I have difficulty breathing.

"Come home, Ted. The children and I will take care of you," Darlene writes a note for Ted.

I hesitate a few seconds.

"You can live with me and Owen," I write. I try to sound definite, firm.

The room grows warmer.

Finally, the social worker writes a sign with big letters. "Which one?" pointing first to his wife, then to me.

Ted blurts out, struggles to speak the words. "Nobody. My son … me … in my apartment." His son Brad is a student in the daytime and loads packages for UPS at night.

Ted's voice sounds like the man I knew and loved before the stroke. Independent, stubborn, strong.

The bidding war is over.

Ted hesitates and then says to Darlene, "Nan…cy will take me to my apartment."

On our way after his discharge, we stop at a neighborhood drugstore to fill his prescriptions, primarily blood pressure medications and an anticoagulent, Coumadin. I worry that Ted might forget to take his medicines. He'll need a schedule.

While we wait for the meds to be filled, we linger outside the store for a breath of air. Traces of dirty snow on the edge of the sidewalk remind us that spring is still a few weeks away. As Ted paces up and down alongside the building, he stops to put a cigarette in his mouth. He reaches into his jacket pocket for a lighter and instead holds a credit card to the cigarette tip, expecting a flame.

He realizes his mistake and we laugh.

We pick up the medicines and drive to his apartment. We enter his place, which smells of beer and cigarettes. It seems a hundred years since he's sat here, night after night, grading papers, smoking, drinking and watching TV.

After picking up clutter in the apartment, I sit down to write out a medicine schedule. Ted must take six prescriptions at specific times during the day. I make a chart with multiple columns, labeling days of the week, times of day, and the names of the prescriptions. I use colored markers, a different color for each medicine. Whoever is the caregiver will initial in the space next to the medicine each time Ted takes it.

Next, I map out a schedule for care—Brad in the late night to late morning, Darlene through the afternoon to early evening, and me for the evening hours.

Later that night, when Brad has left for work, we make love. Ted's afraid he can't perform. I don't care. I just want him to be well.

I just want him.

In upcoming days, I set about organizing the apartment, researching how to help a stroke victim. I leave elaborate notes for Darlene so that when she arrives the next day, she will know what I've done—that the laundry is finished, or not, that the prescriptions need refilling so I have called them in, that I've found a good speech therapist at a local hospital. Some evenings when I arrive for my shift, I find that Darlene has brought over casseroles and other dishes she knows he likes—scalloped potatoes, roast beef. Ted has told me she's a good cook.

Most of the time, he refuses her food.

In his broken sentences, Ted tells me that for the first time in her life, Darlene has started jogging with their daughter. I've worked out at a gym for years. I'm trim and much younger. She must be competing with me. I understand. I would do the same.

At the college, I've noticed that Darlene's fashion has changed. She's worn shorter dresses and skirts, elaborate, multiple chains of beads around her neck, and long, dangling earrings. She smiles constantly, perhaps to will happiness to a face that struggles with humiliation and anger. It seems to me that she was constantly visible, appearing in my pathway in the English department door, or in the hallway when I'm on my way to class.

I try not to think about how it must feel to her, this public exposure of her failed marriage.

Brad's schedule changes to the day shift, so I try to find someone to fill in during the morning and early afternoon. I leave Darlene a note, telling her I've scheduled an appointment with a woman named Agnes who wants the job.

At 11 a.m. on a morning in late February, I arrive early to be ready for Agnes. Brad is home. I'm relieved that he's there.

Suddenly, Darlene walks slowly and deliberately into the living room.

"Good morning, Ted, Brad." She ignores me.

She sets down a box of sugared donuts on the coffee table and goes into the kitchen to make coffee. She does not respond when I say, "Good morning."

Ted sits in a chair with his shoulders hunched and his arms clutching his upper body in a hug. He reminds me of a trapped animal.

"*I'm* going to do the interview," she says, finally looking at me directly. I wonder if some of her friends have urged her to be tough with me, the "other woman," the "marriage breaker."

When Agnes arrives, I try to begin the interview, but Darlene interrupts me and says to Agnes, "*I'm* the one in charge of the interview. *I'm* asking the questions." I notice that Ted has become more agitated. His breathing quickens. He paces back and forth in the living room. His face and neck muscles tighten, and he clears his throat again and again, the nervous habit I know so well.

He's being treated as if he's invisible.

Darlene completes the interview while I sit at the end of the couch. She and Agnes agree to a schedule. I'm not sure if I should leave or stay. But I remember that I've told Ted I will stick by him. As soon as the door closes behind Agnes, I tell Darlene that I want to speak with her in private, in Brad's bedroom.

"You're upsetting Ted. Can't you see that he feels helpless and anxious?"

"You have done a very bad thing, Nancy. You've taken Ted away from me and our children." As she speaks, she moves around the room, her body bent forward slightly toward me, as if she's ready to spring into action.

At this moment, I fear she's right.

But hasn't this marriage been over for years? Hasn't he told me over, and over again? It would be so easy for me to leave now that he's had a stroke. But how can I back down now? I've told him I would stay. By my actions, I've told the world that I'll stick by him.

I leave Darlene and walk back to the living room, where Ted is stretched out on the couch with his eyes closed. She follows.

"I can't do this." I tell Brad. "With this kind of pressure, I can't help your dad."

Brad nods, puts his hands on his mother's shoulders and tells her to leave. I can tell he's trying to be gentle, but firm.

How must he feel, talking to his mother like this?

Darlene looks at him, at Ted, and her shoulders sink.

I just wish she would leave so I don't have to see her like this, so I don't have to feel guilty, so I don't have to ask myself, what am I doing?

IN MARCH, I spend almost every evening with Ted. I work out an arrangement for Cindy, a young woman whose mother runs a day care, to take care of Owen in the evenings.

Owen will be fine, I think. He is resilient, but he's already experienced two other fathers, all because of my unwise decisions and restlessness. When everything is settled and Ted and I are married, it will all be worth it. I'll worry about all of it later.

By late March, the days lengthen, and the Michigan spring sunshine melts the dirty snow. Tension builds between us. One Saturday night when I come in with preparations for dinner, Ted barely greets me. He has that look on his face, a barrier that blocks any light in his eyes. He holds his body like a piece of unfinished wood, stiff and full of splinters. I have no idea what's wrong. I put a chicken in the oven to bake, hoping a nice meal will improve the evening.

As I work in the kitchen, I wonder if his attitude has anything to do with what happened earlier that week. Ted received a credit card bill. Apparently, Darlene had used the card. The day he'd showed me the bill he was angry, worried about expenses since he's on disability pay. When he complained to me about the bill, I asked him if he'd like me to contact his attorney. I wrote him several notes, asking "yes" or "no" questions: "Do you want me to call Mr. __?" *Yes.* "Do you want him to call your lawyer?" *Yes.* Only days before, he had said "Yes. Contact my lawyer." Or at least, this is what I understood him to say to me.

When Ted finally speaks, he tells me in broken sentences that his wife came over with a letter from her lawyer, warning her not to put charges on the card while they are separated. When she came to talk with Ted, she was crying. She blamed me.

"It's her fault. She called my lawyer and told him about the credit card."

For more than an hour, I struggle to communicate with Ted.

I'm sure I can make him understand if I'm patient enough. Is he pretending not to understand while I write note after note, changing the phrasing and emphasis of the sentences to make them clearer?

"Did you tell me to call your lawyer?"

Confused expression.

"Did you not want me to call Darlene's lawyer?" I ask.

No response.

"You told me that you were angry. You said to call your lawyer."

Silence.

"Didn't you want me to call about Darlene's charges?"

He lifts his shoulders as if he doesn't understand.

"Why are you angry?"

More of the same. He acts as if we've never discussed the matter.

I WRITE MORE NOTES, losing any sense of time. When one message doesn't work, I crumble the paper, throw it in the trashcan, and try to write the message a different way.

I'm exhausted. I go into the bedroom to take a nap. I can't sleep. I hear the rustle of paper. I return to the living room to find Ted crawling around on the floor with every one of the little pieces of crumbled paper from the trash can. He's spreading them, stained with chicken fat, on the carpet as if he's working a giant picture puzzle.

He looks at the papers, putting his face close to floor and picking up paper after paper to examine it, and then put it down.

Then he screams at me.

"You mock me! Get out! Get out!"

I start to leave then turn around to grab my pot of chicken from the oven.

I must be responsible, guilty of something horrible.

THE NEXT MORNING, I awake to a knotted stomach and an aching head. I'm exhausted from the weeks of 18–20 hour days preparing for and meeting my classes, grading papers, spending time with Owen to check his homework and talk about his day before going to Ted's for my "night shift," taking care of medicines and medical appointments, and facing the social pressures from stares at work and reactions from Darlene.

It's not worth it anymore. How much brain damage does Ted actually have? I don't know any longer if I'm capable of this commitment. If I got out of the way, would he go back to Darlene?

In the early evening, Brad calls.

"Nancy, where are you? Have you been over here today?"

I don't answer his question. Instead, "I'd be over shortly"

Relief.

He still wants me!

When I enter the apartment, Ted looks bewildered about why I've come so late. He acts as if he's forgotten that he kicked me out last night.

In my journal earlier that month, I'd challenged myself to "maintain the strength I've displayed to date."

I wonder whether I can keep my commitment. I don't yet understand what it is that keeps me coming back in the face of rejection. I don't remember the ways in which, as a child, I tried and tried to please my father. I don't remember that as a girl I craved attention. I just remember that I feel this in my body.

Moving In

22

MAY 1987. Soon after the credit card incident, Ted tells Darlene that he will pursue the divorce. Owen and I now live in a historic apartment in Springwells Park, not far from the house I bought with Evan. Ted will move in when his apartment lease is up.

I like these brick apartments Henry Ford built in the 1930s for his workers. They were renovated in the previous decade and they were a hot item. We live in one of the only two apartments with a fireplace. For me, having a fireplace is a cozy reminder of home. It probably has something to do with my childhood reading of the Bobbsey Twins books or the poem "Snowbound," by John Greenleaf Whittier:

> We piled, with care, our nightly stack
> Of wood against the chimney-back—
> The oaken log, green, huge, and thick,
> And on its top the stout back-stick;
> The knotty forestick laid apart,
> And filled between with curious art
> The ragged brush; then, hovering near,
> We watched the first red blaze appear,
> Heard the sharp crackle, caught the gleam
> On whitewashed wall and sagging beam,
> Until the old, rude-furnished room
> Burst, flower-like, into rosy bloom.

I love our apartment, but this is the same neighborhood where I felt smothered by middle class suburban expectations. I know I will never be a Donna Reed or Betty Crocker. Somehow, in this space, I feel free of those expectations. An apartment is temporary, not as permanent as a house.

Change and permanence, a balancing act.

When Owen is home from school, he and Ted play badminton or shoot baskets at the nearby park. During his college years at a nearby university, Ted was a basketball player and despite the stroke and his heart problem, he is still agile and slim. In a black and white photo from the 1950s, he jumps, suspended in mid-air, his long body lifted toward the ball, as if he's floating or flying.

Though Ted's speech is improving, he can't hear and understand what people are saying. "Their voices sound like whale calls under water," he explains.

My job, as I see it, is to take care of his business, call from friends to make lunch plans and doctor's appointments. I'm happy to be the communicator if it will help Ted get better, but I can tell he is impatient. Before his stroke, he was an independent, proud and stubborn man. Now every ordinary act is a challenge.

Ted's days are simple. He takes walks, stops for coffee and donuts, shoots baskets, and works his Petoskey stones, which he polishes to a shining surface clear enough to see the ancient animals that formed the stone. These stones are actually fossil coral found near Petoskey, in the lower part of the Upper Peninsula. Ted works them on the picnic table he bought and painted a rust red color.

One warm afternoon when I enter my apartment from a shimmering summer afternoon, the blinking light on my answering machine signals a message. I hear Ted's voice, speaking, hesitating, speaking again, to read for me his favorite poem, a medieval lyric:

Western wind, when will thou blow?
The small rain down can rain.
Christ, that my love were in my arms,
And I in my bed again.

As I listen to his voice on tape, I hear his effort, the exercise of a determined and stubborn man. He wants so very much to speak again. He wants to go back to teaching.

His voice fills me with a longing, an ache for his recovery.

If he holds on, I can help him.

We spend a peaceful summer. Owen visits his dad in Alabama, and I teach an English class. We have time together like a normal couple.

Fall comes, and Ted's divorce date is set.

THE DAYS BEFORE his appearance in divorce court, Ted doesn't want to see me. He says he needs time alone to think about the end of this long marriage.

In my journal of September 14, his court date, I write:

What strikes me as odd about this moment in time is that I sit anesthetizing myself against the conclusions that this day will bring. Certainly Ted's "day in court" has brought fears in both of us to the surface. He's withdrawn, and he's been cold and silent. I'm in a panic and rage over his reaction. I know I'll survive whatever conclusion the day brings, but I so want the continuing peace that I have felt in his presence over the last lovely weeks of this summer. Be it a disastrous failure or reversal, or an act of incision and competition today, the results ring out tragic possibilities for all—Owen, Ted's family—and even, yes, Ted. He is strong, has survived much, but can he survive this final breaking away from patterns that have run his life for a long time? His withdrawal from me suggests an old pattern, as does my panic and rage.

My pain lies in the hard question to myself: Have I been ethical in "helping" with this divorce? Should I have stayed out, withdrawn after his stroke, allowed Ted to make his own way back to D? Have I really destroyed a family, as Darlene accused, even though Ted made his own decision to stay with me?

In court, Ted is able to respond to the judge's questions. His divorce goes through. Now we can build a life.

IN DECEMBER, we celebrate Christmas with my mother in Alabama, and we make it back in time for Ted's sister's Christmas party on Christmas night. All of the siblings are there, and their spouses, including his brother Dan, who likes to drink and enjoys touching and kissing women behind doors or in corners when he thinks no one was looking. I avoid him as much as possible, but he does manage one squeeze of my backside as I walk by him.

Owen, who is seven years old, plays ping-pong with some of Ted's boy relatives. I hear quarreling, a tearful voice, and then Owen screams, "You can't do that, you jerk!" We leave soon after, but inside my Subaru, Ted turns around to Owen from the front seat and yells at him. I can't exactly make out what he says to my son. His words are garbled and angry. He seems to be scolding Owen for misbehaving. Owen pulls his winter coat tight around him against the cold.

THE FIRST THREE MONTHS of 1988 slide by without incident, as Owen, Ted and I settle in to live as a family. Ted reads newspapers, shoots baskets at a local gym, and goes out to breakfast most mornings. Owen attends the private school he's been in since kindergarten, and as the spring approaches, he practices soccer with a city team. Once or twice a week Ted and I attend games either in or out of town to watch Owen play defense, running like a gazelle down the field to return a ball before it goes too deep into his team's territory. In my study next to our bedroom, I grade papers and work on research. Every once in a while, I pause to look out of the bay window at the neatly mowed lawn as it turns from dead brown to green with the changing seasons.

Ted's drinking increases to six or seven beers a day. He smokes more. His fifty-eighth birthday approaches. I'm worried about his health, so I mention something to him about his habits and his health.

"This relationship is over," he says as he walks out the door.

Over the next few days, I take Owen to school and I go to work, coming home to stare into the cold fireplace. I buy a pack of cigarettes and one night, while smoking and drinking wine, I burn a hole in the beige sectional couch I bought with Evan. That night and for several nights, I try smoking until my throat is raw and my breath stinks like rotting food.

I'm punishing myself.

In my journal two days before Ted's birthday on March 12, I write to understand what is happening.

> *Odd how long it's been since I entered anything in this journal. It seems to take a crisis for me to use this method. Ted is almost moved in, and is now, today, moving out—books, typewriter—all that he's already moved into the apartment. He's leaving because I had to be honest about the drinking he was doing as he prepared to live with us. I thought his drinking was sabotaging the move. When I confronted him, I touched a nerve and he wanted out immediately. If life were fair, he would acknowledge my efforts at growth. What I wish—all I can possibly expect—is that I see whatever happens now between us as realistically as possible.*
>
> *One great and absolute truth for me: Unless I deal with the problems, there will be no chance whatever for a decent relationship. There will be dependency of the unhealthy sort. I will pussyfoot and lie and be untrue to myself.*
>
> *The die is cast.*

ON TED'S BIRTHDAY, March 12, we schedule a meeting to discuss our problems. He is to arrive at the apartment at 3:00 p.m., so I prepare a long list of statements and questions. Twenty years today since Dad's death, I write. A day for reflection, for coming together, for revelation, for truth. God give me the strength to face it!

In my head, I accuse Ted, supporting my own "truth of heart" and chastising him for misleading me to believe we were going to be together.

When I answer the door at 3:00 p.m. sharp, Ted stands on the porch, looking again like a splintered two-by-four. His face is impassive.

I long for him even as I see him. I want him to come back.

We sit at the dining room to talk. "We need to communicate. I wanted to be able to speak my mind to you without tiptoeing around land mines." I speak to his silence.

That's what he's done, I realize. By walking out and staying away for days without a word, he's punished me for confronting him and his habits.

"With you, there is no negotiation. There is only your decision," I say.

Ted listens to my list, looking at my paper while following the words with his eyes. He finally speaks. I feel as if I'm in a court of law

"I won't stand for nagging about my beer and cigarettes. Darlene nagged like that.

I won't live with it again."

I want someone who won't be too easy. When I saw him in the doorway, my body cried out for roughness, even punishment.

The next day, he moves his boxes of books back into the apartment.

Our lovemaking is more intense than ever.

Forever

23

ON JUNE 14, 1988, my forty-second birthday, Ted and I enter Judge Joseph Burtell's courtroom, Nineteenth District Court, Dearborn, Michigan.

My fourth wedding. One last time. This has to be it. I'm finally conquering my restlessness with a partner who will keep me on edge. I wanted someone who is not easy. Now I have him.

Today Ted looks unusually formal, since he's most often in jeans, a t-shirt and tennis shoes. He's dressed in his blue pinstripe "wedding and funeral suit," as he calls it. I wear a two-piece suit in a peach color with tiny artificial pearls around the neckline, a matching pearl comb, triple pearls in my ears, a string of small pearls around my neck that had been a gift from my mother for my first wedding some twenty-two years earlier, and a pearl ring. Pearls are my birthstone and a strong reminder of life origins, the sea and sand.

The small room seems suddenly smaller as we stand near the judge with Owen, two couples who are witnesses, and Ted's brother and sister-in-law. The sounds of traffic outside on the main thoroughfare, Michigan Avenue, fade as we begin the simple service.

We've adapted our vows from a ceremony the judge provided. Ted struggles to articulate the words, but he makes no mistakes. Then I read a poem I've written just for him. It's about a home place, about nurturing, and safety, and love. About the body, and the spirit, and roots.

You are the roadway
I thought I had taken before
But wound around,
        confused—
Touching the familiar bark of a tree
I thought was guiding me
until I stumbled back onto my path,
        in the dark.

You are the beam ahead,
        A warming light,
A white heat like the sun rising above at noon
I feel your hot fire.

You are the cottage filled with warm smells—
Jasmine, honey, and cinnamon,
the fire aglow in the heart place.

I am coming home.

I marry one last time. It's got to work.

ON OWEN'S BIRTHDAY, October 9, we move into a small brick bungalow in West Dearborn. Even with the tensions of moving and my recent absence while attending a conference, I think I'll be happy in here. It will stay clean, free of the stench of nicotine. Ted has agreed to smoke only in the basement. And the house has a wood-burning fireplace.

This is the house where I will greet Ted on that freezing winter's night, lipstick smeared on his face. But for now, we are happy to have an official, legal status between us. Maybe people will stop looking at me as the "other woman." It's been a long haul to get past departmental disapproval, Ted's stroke, and our divorces, especially his, because of how complicated it was. Now at last I can say that I'm Ted's wife. No arguments about credit cards and money. After all, I make my own decent salary and can pay my share of the expenses.

We divide the household expenses on a 60/40 basis, with me paying 60 percent. Ted's long-term disability pay is less than his regular salary. When he turns sixty-five on March 12, 1995, he will split his pension 50/50 with Darlene. It's the law.

WE SETTLE INTO THE NEIGHBORHOOD, and Owen makes friends with three boys who live down the street. They run back and forth constantly between our houses. They laugh, argue, and play basketball on the driveway. Boy stuff.

In the spring of 1989, Ted and I plant a garden of vegetables in the back yard beside the garage. He constructs a frame structure of wood to let the green, rich vines of zucchini, green beans, and yellow squash weave upward toward the sunny sky. Cucumbers and tomato vines crawl over the earth below.

Ted builds a wire fence around plants to protect them from the rabbits that hop around in our back yard and from the neighborhood raccoon that turns over trash cans in the middle of the night.

I move into a routine with my teaching and research, and Ted takes over most of the housekeeping chores, since he's not returned to work.

BY THE SUMMER OF 1989, the speech therapists tell me that Ted has reached a plateau, and unless he allows them to use other techniques, he will remain where he is, able to hear some words, but mostly receiving information by hand gesture, tone of voice, and the written word.

He will never teach again, they say.

For several months, I've researched music therapy for brain damage. I understand that Ted's left brain, where his language and reasoning skills live, has suffered significant damage. I also understand that music and creativity live in the right brain. If language is combined with music, the right brain can take over some of the skills destroyed with the left brain's cells. Words, coupled with music, could prompt his right brain to work with language.

I'm excited about my discoveries and even give Ted an audio tape to stimulate right brain activity.

One afternoon he enters the side door into the kitchen to tell me the news. "I'm quitting speech therapy."

I tell him about my research on music therapy. He refuses to pursue it.

"Enough of that bullshit!"

That's the end of it.

TED WORKS EVERY DAY on his Petoskey stones. He polishes them with various grades of sandpaper and a fine powder, and finally with his hands. I find comfort in the regularity and rhythm of his polishing. It's like meditation.

On one cool fall afternoon, I drive into the garage to see Ted sitting at the red picnic table, working his stones. A baseball cap covers his bald head, and his bristly beard, grey and black, shifts with the motions of his pursing lips as he draws on a cigarette. In jeans and sweatshirt, from the back he looks like a much younger man. The makings of his craft are a dishpan filled with powdery water to wash the forming stones and the sandpaper, which he applies again and again. His art has become alchemy. His hands, long fingers roughened with the process, work the stones, work them again, patiently and stubbornly. Before his stroke, he told me, "I love to find the life of each stone, the history of each of these five-sided animals, who bonded themselves together millions of years ago. I want to bring them to life again, after all of these centuries. I'm touching history."

151

And I can see you, stone in hand
in the sunlight,
      polishing, polishing,
caressing the rough rock until,
with no labor lost, its
smooth skin shines
in your brown hand—
Your dark face,
      intent on the task,
finds your work is done
when holding it smooth and gleaming
against the rays of sun to look upon
      and touch.

Today, I treasure all of the stones he gave to us—the large, flat one, the round one that had another kind of fossil on the other side, the one he polished and carved into the shape of an arrowhead for Owen.

Eclipse
24

AFTER THE SPEECH THERAPY ends, Ted drinks heavily. He chain-smokes in our basement, where he sits watching TV in the usual sweatshirt, jeans, and baseball cap, working a stone in his hand. The entire house reeks of stale smoke. When my friend Sue stops by to take a walk with me, she comments that she can smell the smoke as I open the door. Owen showers in the basement every morning, and he complains about walking through a stinky room. Even in the faculty lounge at the college, a colleague standing ten feet away from me asks if someone is smoking. Though I don't realize it, I'm carrying the stench on my clothing, in my skin. I can't escape Ted's habit.

It's like Dad in a darkened room, the black and white television blaring, the smell of nicotine. Smoke coated the walls and furniture. So familiar. Even when Marge and Rob had their first child, they still smoked. We'd all gather in Robbie's room. Here was a vulnerable infant, a new baby, in a crib sleeping, with the family gathered around. The smoke permeated the air of that little bedroom. An attack on young, new lungs.

IN LATE SUMMER OF 1989, Ted, Owen and I plan a family trip to Alabama. The night before we are to leave, the news reports an eclipse of the moon. I hear the voices of excited children and adults gathered on the sidewalk, looking toward the sky. They wait for the few minutes when the earth will move through its orbit between the moon and the sun.

I come inside for a minute, leaving behind the excitement on the street to check on laundry I'm washing for the trip.

I find Ted on his high stool in the basement, in front of the washing machine, his back to me, open beer can on the washer. As usual, he's working his Petoskey stones. He doesn't turn around.

"I'm not going with you and Owen tomorrow. I want a divorce."

I struggle to keep my voice steady.

"I'm sorry you feel this way."

I've learned not to react.

I kiss him on the cheek and go outdoors to watch the eclipse.

The next morning before Owen and I leave, I sit down with Ted at our dining room table. This is like a war council, or a union negotiation. Armed with paper and pen, I ask him exactly why he wants the divorce. The sunshine filters through the window, speckled with leaf patterns. On this clear, warm morning, he's unable explain himself.

It's clear to me that Ted is playing a game. He talks about some dispute between Owen and his friends the day before. Ted was helpless to intervene because he couldn't understand what they were saying. It's clear to me he doesn't want a divorce, but he wants to make a point.

Why don't I just say 'Yes, I'll give you a divorce'? Why don't I get out of this while I can?

But I'm not ready. I still think I can help. And I should stay. It's the right thing to do. Quitting is something I've done too much of.

And maybe there'll be a miracle.

But I grow weary of games.

THE AA LITERATURE tells me that one shouldn't drink with an alcoholic. It's called "codependency," and all it does is validate the alcoholic's habit. I determine I will have no wine with dinner. I refuse offers of a beer from Ted's stash in the old refrigerator in the basement. I'm determined not to support his habit.

He can drink alone, at least here in the house. I won't play that game.

OWEN AND I BEGIN the familiar drive to Alabama, down I-75 and then 71 to LaGrange, Kentucky, the first day. Then we pick up I-65 in Nashville and head toward Hartselle, Alabama, my hometown where I went to high school, and for many summers, where my family visited Mama and Papa Steve. Two days on the road. A relief from a constant vigilance about what I say, a constant effort to stay calm and firm.

When Owen and I are not talking, I have plenty of time to think. Ted believes all is well between us, that we made up from last night's, what shall I call it? Divorce threat? There was no clear reason why he talked about divorce, other than to punish me, to keep me on edge. Is he jealous of my life outside our marriage?

As I drive through Ohio, I think of our parting this morning. With the car packed for the trip, the three of us had breakfast at a neighborhood restaurant. The conversation was loving, and Ted said he would miss us. Because he wanted some exercise, after breakfast I let him out a few blocks from our house. He walked along the neighborhood streets, where an early Michigan cold snap had caused leaves to begin turning gold, orange, and rust. He walked through some fallen leaves, turning around every minute or two to wave goodbye. I was sad. Something had changed inside of me.

Why did I marry him? I wanted to help him, like I wanted to help Dad. It isn't working. I have to start living my own life, separate from his.

As much as the idea of being alone frightens me, I think about Owen, the little boy who has experienced three fathers already. I think of how I've tried to create a bond, a consistent relationship, with my son.

I left Bill when my son was a baby. Owen and I were a team, like Helen Reddy's lyrics to "Song to Jeffrey." It had always been us "against the world."

I'd been there for my son. Sometimes it was rough.

There are stories I can't relate now, for this memoir is not his story. Yet he's clearly and integrally a part of the story I'm telling.

I still struggle with the guilt of the unsettled life I gave him in his early years.

MY FIRST WINTER ALONE with my baby Owen was 1981–82, only months after I was divorced from his father and began my new job at the college.

From our large window to the west, in this new apartment in Westland, we have a view of the natural woods above the Rouge River. This section is a nature park, untouched except for trails. We watch trees change with the season. In spring and summer, I take Owen down to the trail through the woods above this slow tickle of the river. He learns to walk shortly after we move into the apartment, and on those beautiful days, he will run ahead of me, using up his energy on the uneven path.

These heavy, fierce winters of the early 1980s bring sub-zero temperatures and deep drifts of snow. Owen runs among crystalline ice sculptures of the trees. Their curved branches arch over our heads like lace. He peeks around a tree at me, playing hide-and-seek. When he stands behind the tree, I hear him suppress a giggle.

Because of a blizzard, we spend an entire weekend inside, until Sunday. After the strong winds stop, I dress Owen in a blue snowsuit with matching booties and furry hood, an appliqué of the Beatrix Potter bunny on the front. His grandmother M.M. gave it to him for his first Christmas. Owen walks gingerly in the snow, piled deep above his knees, and then he falls on his bottom. He looks surprised. In the fierce cold we try to roll balls of snow and make a snowman, but when the wind picks up and stings our faces, we hurry indoors.

After shedding cold, icy clothing, we have a cup of hot chocolate and play with his Legos or a puzzle. Later that night, after I give him his bath and dress him in footie pajamas, I put on the record of children's songs by Peter, Paul, and Mary, and as we do many nights, I rock Owen to sleep while I sing along with "Puff the Magic Dragon." I hold him to my chest, encircle him with my arms and smell his blond curls, slightly damp and fresh with baby shampoo.

Not unlike my life in the military with its changes and upheavals, Owen and I have managed to survive our own changes and upheavals.

Now as we drive alone to Alabama, he is nine years old. With pain in my chest, I know that if we have to, we'll make another big change.

DURING THE DRIVE, Owen and I talk about getting back home, about all we have to do to get him, and me, ready for school this fall. We do not talk about Ted, but in moments of silence, I remember the good things, the love and energy Ted has put into our marriage. I remember how up and down it has been, how one day never looks like the next one.

A journal entry in early 1989:

> *A one-day-at-a-time approach is best, especially since I do believe Ted is an alcoholic. He drinks heavily during the Detroit Pistons games as a reward for his hard work.*
>
> *I hate the excess, but I love the man.*
>
> *What is so exciting about Ted is his energy. Tonight our furnace is out and he has brought inside two extra loads of wood ready for the fire. As if we are on a great adventure!*
>
> *Sometimes, I feel overwhelmed with our life together. Then I return to one day at a time, and I remember his goodness.*

ON WINTER AFTERNOONS, I arrive home to hear the sound of wood splitting in the garage. Every day now, Ted positions a large block of wood on a tree stump and brings down the axe hard, recalling Thoreau's *Walden*: "I played about the stumps...they warmed me twice—once while I was splitting them, and again when they were on the fire, so that no fuel could give out more heat."

Ted's chopping is steady, a comforting daily rhythm. After stacking the wood in neat piles in the backyard, Ted brings in a load and builds a fire in the fireplace for me, waiting only for my match to create a burst of warmth.

On one of Owen's birthdays, Ted brings home a new red bike. Halting every few seconds to find the words, he explains how he went to Sears to buy the bike. How he struggled to tell the salesman what he wanted, searching for the words as he tried to speak. Ted pointed to his ears and then brought out a small tablet of paper and a pencil. He wrote notes to the salesman and asked him to write back.

It took a long time, probably one and a half hours, for them to find the right bike and complete the purchase.

When Owen sees the bike, he yells out in excitement and takes off into the neighborhood, the bike pedals whirling like a pinwheel.

On Owen's ninth birthday, Ted gives him two checkbook boxes of one-dollar bills—$500 total—that he's collected over the last year. A photo of the two of them shows Owen smiling down at the thick stack of green bills. Ted has his arm around Owen's shoulders.

ON THE DRIVE BACK from Alabama, I tell myself that Ted has been the best father he could be to Owen. He's played basketball with him, watched him play soccer. But I know Ted is not well. I can't deny it any longer. The damage of the stroke limited what he can do, how much he can help Owen in the upcoming years. And there was the drinking, the addictive behavior, and his efforts to pull me into codependency games with guilt.

Soon Owen will grow from a boy to a young man. He will need encouragement, a male role model. As much as I've tried, I've failed to make a lasting and solid family relationship for my son. I've wanted stability. Continuity. A vibrant relationship

I've failed.

More Games

25

ALL OF THOSE YEARS my dad drank, no one really talked to me about it. When his men carried him upstairs that afternoon, nobody told me, the child, what was happening. My sister Betty was angry and detached, Mom said nothing, and Marge glossed over problems by playing games with me. Only years later did Mom tell me that the doctor recommended she give Dad small amounts of whiskey every day, starting with a tablespoon and reducing the amount until he wasn't drinking any alcohol. This idea seems absurd today, but in the1940s and 1950s, no one thought of alcoholism as a disease. It was moral failure, not addiction. No one recognized coping as co-dependency: *Give him what he wants. Push him out of sight when we have company. Even though there's an elephant in the living room, don't talk about it, even to your close friends, and certainly not to people who work with or above you. It's a disgrace.*

One story pre-dates my memory, a story my sister Betty told me decades later, when I was a grown woman. We were talking about Dad's problems and all of the things I couldn't remember.

One night, Dad was drunk and sat down next to my crib when I was asleep. I must have been one year old, or younger. He had a gun. He told my mom and sisters that he was going to shoot me, and then shoot himself. Betty says she went over and picked up the gun. She put it under her mattress, where it stayed for months. She's not sure how she stayed so calm. As far as I know, no one discussed it with Dad later.

What anguish my mother and sisters must have endured. They were helpless to do anything for him. What anguish he must have had to want to end the life of his infant child and his own.

And for my mother, divorce was never an option.

WHEN OWEN AND I RETURN from our Southern trip, we launch into the new school year. I push aside my doubts about my marriage to Ted, always hoping the problems will solve themselves. This wasn't exactly the same elephant that lived with my family during Dad's drinking days, but it feels familiar, like change and movement I experienced when I was young. In the Army, we would be settled, and suddenly, we would have to leave home, school, and friends, to move to another military assignment. The message was, *you can't have too much stability, too much security. You must keep moving. Keeps life exciting and challenging.* In this marriage, I've learned to deal with surprises and disruptions I couldn't predict, just like the new assignments in the Army.

During the fall term, I attend meetings for over a month with a hiring committee for our college academic dean. I haven't cooked much lately.

One evening soon after the committee work is done, I decide to make a special dinner of tacos because Owen loves them. Tonight, I'm relieved that the intense work of hiring is over. I'm happy in the kitchen, grilling beef, grating cheese, and chopping tomatoes and lettuce. I place the dishes on our table, along with warmed shells, guacamole and salsa, and call Owen and Ted to dinner. Owen sits down quickly and begins to fill his plate with food. Ted also sits down, but he stares at the food like it's poison—he's still and silent a moment, until he begins to shout.

"I'm not eating this. You know I hate Mexican food. I'm going out to dinner!"

161

Ted leaves the house, slams the side door closed. I watch his brown Escort back out of the driveway while he clenches a lit cigarette tightly between his lips.

He's angry because I've been preoccupied with work. He once had a full career of teaching and union work, and now he can't teach. Ever.

When he comes home later, he says nothing. We never discuss the incident, but I'm on my toes every day, waiting for more eruptions. I don't like it. Instead of working out problems by communicating, Ted puts me between the rock of anger and the hard place of silence. *How are we supposed to work out problems if we don't talk?*

On another afternoon, I arrive home to see Ted in the back yard, working on his stones at the red picnic table, an open beer sitting next to him on the picnic table. I leave my car and walk to greet him. I'm wearing a short skirt that shows my knees. He stares at me (I'd call it ogling) as I approach, and his eyes run up and down my body. I feel I'm being undressed in my own back yard by my own husband. I feel like an object. I ignore his glance and turn away toward the house.

I am not one of your topless friends. I won't be treated like a cheap whore.

That night I prepare foods that Ted likes—pork chops, salad, and baked potato. Perhaps I want to make up for the tacos incident. Close to dinnertime, he enters the side door only long enough to speak.

"I'm going out for dinner."

He turns and walks out of the house.

I think I'm supposed to feel guilty.

I remind myself that a stroke victim has lost much personal power. Maybe Ted needs to exert power whenever he can.

FOOD IS OFTEN AN ISSUE for Ted when he's unhappy about something else. I've been reading about alcoholic games, and these food battles fit the pattern. I've learned that the alcoholic is very good at staging incidents over nothing. He creates excuses to fight, excuses to erupt in anger.

I resolve not to play the games, but I struggle with guilt and responsibility. *Why didn't I see this pattern before we married? I think I must have longed for Ted so badly, that I would have done anything to keep him. I wanted to help him conquer his problems.*

Before we married, I didn't draw the right conclusions. I was too desperate to have him. And I didn't want to think about how paranoid he could be. I chose not to remember a conference I attended in Nebraska, in 1986, before we married.

AFTER CHECKING IN at the hotel, I call Ted at his apartment. I want to make sure everything was okay with him before I allow myself to relax and enjoy seeing old friends.

Ted answers the phone, his voice deep, echoing, as if from a deep cave.

"Hello, Ted. I just wanted you to know I'm here safely. How is everything?" I speak slowly into the phone so he can understand.

"Who is he? Who is the man you are sleeping with?" I pause a minute. I don't understand what he means.

"What do you mean?"

"Who is the man you're sleeping with? Who answered the phone at the hotel?"

"I don't know what you are talking about. I just checked in and wanted to see if you were okay before I went downstairs to registration." I'm anxious and have to remind myself to speak slowly. Silence. He's waiting for an explanation.

"I don't understand what you said to me," he continues, his voice dropping even lower. This is an easy explanation for almost any misunderstanding we have—Ted says he can't understand what I'm saying to him. I remember the incident with Darlene and the credit card, my notes spotted with chicken grease, spread out on the floor, his insistence that he remembered nothing about telling me to call the lawyer.

With the phone to my ear, I feel my stomach clinch. I sit down on the bed to steady myself.

I'm guiding a canoe over steep rapids and it's about to flip over.

Ted hangs up on me, so I decide to go downstairs to the conference area. It's hard to relax. In the midst of hugs and greetings from friends, I keep thinking about the conversation.

Later in the evening, I attend a party of several people from Sioux Falls, people I worked with during my summer research project. I leave the party briefly to call Ted again from my room. Finally, after ten or twelve rings, he answers, speaking in a voice I can barely hear.

"Hi, I'm calling to see if you're okay. What's wrong? You sound ill or upset."

At that moment, my friend Art sticks his head in my door and says "Nancy, are you coming to the party?"

"Is that him? Is that the man?" Ted asks.

"I don't know what you are talking about. This is my friend from Sioux Falls."

Ted hangs up on me again.

Later that night and for the next two days, I call him again and again. He does not answer. Finally, I decide to enjoy the conference, but my mind keeps turning back to Ted and this misunderstanding. Or is it manipulation?

On Saturday morning, I call him one more time to confirm that he'll pick me up from the plane that night. He finally answers.

"Yes, I'll be there, but our relationship is over." *Click.*

In Detroit as I exit the gate from my airplane, I see Ted standing at the back of the waiting crowd dressed in jeans and a sweatshirt. His arms are folded over his chest, and despite his casual attire, he looks like a disgruntled high school principal waiting to speak to a wayward student. I can imagine his foot tapping.

As I come closer, I notice he has a new haircut. He looks almost boyish, pure.

He looks sober.

As we talk briefly, he seems to be waiting for me to explain my "infidelity."

164

After delaying a few minutes, he finally tells me that when he called the hotel, the male desk clerk answered, and he thought the clerk was my lover. He realized his mistake.

He could have told me sooner, instead of ruining my conference. But he wants to control me.

We collect my bags and drive to Ted's apartment. I notice it's spotless, with fresh soap in the bathroom and fresh sheets on the bed, as if he's cleaned everything for my return.

He never intended to end our relationship. He wants me to be off balance.

We go out to dinner at a local restaurant, and then came home to lie down together. He is eager to be inside of me and I comply.

I am, so to speak, back home.

Somehow, despite feeling chastised wrongly, I'm turned on.

BUT AS TIME PASSES, I cease to play these alcoholic games.

In early November 1990, I plan a Sunday family trip to the Stratford, Ontario Shakespeare Festival for Ted, Owen, and me. We will see the last play of the season. We know that Stratford is in a snow belt and that there's a good chance we will encounter snow on the way back after dark. I don't worry. Ted will be with us.

Late on Saturday night, past midnight, Ted walks upstairs from the basement to continue a conversation we had earlier about purchasing a humidifier for the house. He's been watching TV and drinking. I'm weary from the tedium of communicating by pen and paper. My lower back aches with the effort I've made to lean forward and frame my words carefully so that Ted can try to read my lips. I just want to sleep so we can get a fresh start in the morning.

"Do you really want to spend $300 on a humidifier?" I ask in the midst of dozing. I should say, "Could we discuss the humidifier later?" but my mind and my defense mechanisms have shut down for the day.

"You're being curt with me. Curt, curt, curt!" His mouth bites the end of the word "curt" every time he says it, as if he enjoys spitting it out.

Then, the announcement of my "sentence."

"I won't be going with you and Owen tomorrow."

It's happening again. He's picked a fight for no reason, because he doesn't want to go to Stratford with us. Like the Epiphany dinner. Like the trip to Alabama the day after the eclipse.

It's clear that Ted's looking for an excuse not to go. Maybe he's afraid that he won't understand the play.

"That's fine, Ted. Owen and I will go alone. It's okay."

I work hard to speak calmly, despite my knotted stomach.

I turn out the light, turn over, and curl into a fetal position. *I will not react. I will not be co-dependent and play the game.*

But Ted does not leave the room. He bends over me as I try to curl up tighter. I smell the acrid odor of cigarettes, beer, on his breath and clothing. My body, which was relaxed minutes ago, becomes tense, and my neck and back tighten.

"I don't think you understand me! I am not going with you."

He's screaming this time, and with every word, he spits a spray of beer on my face and head.

He wants me to beg him.

I raise my voice, as if it will help him to understand me.

"That's fine. Owen and I will go alone. Now I'd like to sleep."

When he finally leaves me alone, I climb the stairs to sleep in the guest bed at the other end of Owen's room. My son stirs in his sleep. He probably heard Ted's shouting downstairs.

The next morning Owen and I leave for Stratford without speaking to Ted. All day long, I try to put aside the ugliness of the night before. We eat an elegant lunch at Rundles overlooking the Avon River. It's a grey Canadian winter day, overcast and cold, and the swans that swim here in summer have been taken to their winter home. After lunch, we walk along the river until our noses and fingers are freezing. At 2:00 p.m., we enter the Festival Theater, the first structure built in Stratford for theatrical performances. The building sits on a hill above the curving road and pedestrian walk by the river. Its presence adds to the special experience of being in this town devoted to the finest theater in North America. That afternoon

Owen and I see *Macbeth* with Brian Bedford, famed Stratford actor, playing the main role.

During the performance, I'm able to forget about problems at home.

The play is over at 5:30 p.m., and darkness has already set in when we walk to our car. We begin our three-hour drive back to Dearborn. Snow blows directly into the windshield, so that I can hardly see the road, much less directional and road signs. As we approach signs for King's Highway 101, I take a wrong turn and pick up 103 instead, which will take us a longer way across Ontario, through London, and into Sarnia, where the bridge will lead us back into the States to Port Huron. At the time, I think we are lost. I don't realize that we are on an alternate route. The drive seems endless, and we were cut off from contact, snow blowing directly into our vision of the road. I know that if something happens, I'll be stuck in the car, at night, in a blizzard, with my young son.

Driving through London looking for gas stations on this stormy Sunday night, we see deserted city streets and sparse lights from closed department stores. We continue to Sarnia, then Port Huron, and on to Detroit. The roads clear up steadily as we drive further away from the Ontario Snow Belt.

When we arrive home, we are both exhausted from the strain of the road. Inside the house, the TV blares in the basement. The rooms of the main floor stink of smoke. Owen climbs to his room to do homework. I go to bed upstairs again, exhausted from the strain of driving 150 miles against blinding snow, and from the tension of the night before. I fall asleep quickly.

The next day, neither Ted nor I discuss the incident. Instead, for a day or two, we pass each other in the house, going through the motions of taking out the trash and cooking dinner, washing dishes and vacuuming.

It seems that we are walking down parallel paths which rarely cross. And when they do, the crossing is bitter with regret and anger.

Even With My Mother
26

MORGAN COUNTY, ALABAMA, where my mother lives, has been "dry" (sales and consumption of alcohol are illegal) since well before my dad's drinking days. A recent local election maintained the dry status of the town of Hartselle—no sales of alcohol and supposedly no consumption. You had to drive five miles down Highway 31 toward Decatur to buy your booze. Only five miles there. Only five miles back.

Christmas 1992. Ted, Owen and I begin the two-day drive to Alabama with plans to spend Christmas Eve night at the motel in Nashville, Tennessee. In our room after dinner, Ted consumes a six-pack of beer after he's been to the motel bar. He's silent as he drinks and watches TV. There's tension in the room. I wonder if this steady drinking is some kind of message, a build-up to our visit with my mother.

On Christmas morning, we leave early to reach my mother's home in time to exchange presents. I notice that the closer we came to the Alabama line, the more tense Ted becomes, as if he's been forced to take this trip, as if he would like to be anywhere else other than in a small town in Alabama, in a dry county, on Christmas holiday.

Anywhere but with me, my mother, and my son.

Throughout the Christmas ritual of opening presents and eating at my mother's house, Ted acts like a pouting child. After dinner, he sits on my mother's living room couch and stares at whoever comes into the room. He doesn't try to talk, and when I become desperate to break through his wall of silence, I ask him if he wants to drive the five miles to Decatur to get beer. "No" is all he says.

Mom has asked him not to smoke in the house, but when I climb to our upstairs bedroom, I'm greeted by the stench of burning nicotine.

By December 27, I'm sorry I've brought him with me. I've experienced plenty of stressful Christmases, especially when Dad was gone in the Army. I missed Dad then, felt a hole in our home when he wasn't there. Today, I *want* Ted to disappear.

I've taken Owen to Birmingham to visit with his other grandmother, his father Bill and his wife, his aunt and uncle. That leaves only me and my eighty-seven-year-old mother to deal with Ted.

On Friday night, the three of us sit down to dinner. Mom has made fried chicken with mashed potatoes and gravy in an attempt, she tells me, to make Ted feel special. Ted has hardly spoken all day.

"Would you like gravy on your potatoes?" I ask him.

"You're being curt!"

There's that word again, *curt*. He uses it as a weapon when he's unhappy about something.

I glance at my mother. She sits at her place with a plate full of food, but she isn't eating. I won't blame her if she walks out of her own kitchen, leaving the chicken, potatoes and gravy to cool, become gelatinous on her plate. Instead, she sits looking somewhere else, maybe into the past.

A memory from my childhood in Lafayette flashes in front of me. Mom hunches over her cup of coffee, staring at the space in front of her. Dad is drunk. And there's that feeling again, that vague ache, a pain in my stomach that tells me things are not okay.

No one talks about it.

The next day I drive to Birmingham to visit friends. I need to get away from Ted, to relax and have some fun on this trip. Mom has plans with friends, so Ted will have to sit in her house alone.

Let him lie in the bed he made.

MY DAY IS HAPPY, a visit to a city I love. Birmingham at twilight, nestled in its valley, looks like a bowl of sparkling jewels. During the day, I drop by to see several old friends, talking easily, not worrying that everything I say will be misinterpreted or distorted, not having to constantly interpret. I visit Mary Jane, a musician who gave me a place to stay when I was lonely after divorcing Henry. I see Glenda, a sorority sister, and her husband Pat, and then Helen, my college French teacher who has been a friend since she housed me after I left Henry, some twenty years ago. With these friends, I am honest.

"I don't think this marriage will last. I've tried as hard as I know how. The disability and addictions are too much to deal with," I tell Mary Jane.

"You're a survivor, Nancy. You'll figure it out," she says.

Later in the day, I return with Owen over the sixty-five miles from Birmingham to Hartselle on the dark interstate that I know well from my trips between college and home. We don't speak about what I'm thinking. At twelve years old, he doesn't need my problems.

When we enter the house, Ted is sitting motionless and quiet on the living room couch, just as he was when I left ten hours earlier. Has he moved at all?

Mom lives in a rented house across the street from the owners, the Beasleys. They have become her friends, and Kitty Beasley and Mom study authors together—Whitman, Dickinson, Sexton, Frost, Wordsworth, and Longfellow. Mom loves poetry, and their study keeps her mind alert. The next morning when Larry Beasley drops by to check on the furnace before church, Ted doesn't speak to him, only nods when introduced.

We have breakfast in Mom's little kitchen. We sit for a few minutes at the breakfast table after eating Mom's scrambled eggs, bacon, and her fluffy southern biscuits, the same recipe she made for Dad all of those dark mornings, when after his retirement, he got up at 4:00 a.m. to go to work at Davis-Hunt Cotton Company. We sip coffee, and I taste the last remnants of a biscuit sopping in a mixture of syrup and butter called "goo" by Marge and Papa Steve. I'm thinking about the years of breakfasts with family.

"When are we leaving?" Ted asks my mother. He gazes straight past me at her, as if I'm not there.

"I told you several times that we would be leaving tomorrow, Monday morning." As I speak, I lean over in front of Mom so he has to look me in the face.

"You're being curt again. I'm leaving on the bus," he yells into the small kitchen that only seconds ago had been comfortable and warm.

"Wait a minute, Ted. I'll call and get the bus schedule." *I feel relief when I say it. Let him get the hell out of here.*

I check the yellow pages for the number. I call the station, and then write down the departures of buses from Hartselle to Detroit with a bus change in Nashville. I offer to drop him off at the bus station.

I want him to go. I'm sick of his games. He's done everything he can to sully my mother's home with his pouting and anger, his stinking cigarettes. He's tried to ruin our Christmas.

On Monday, we leave Mom's house on the way back to Michigan. Unfortunately, Ted is still with us.

A MONTH OR SO before Christmas, I had found out that my first husband, Henry, had died. One cold and overcast afternoon in November, I came home from teaching my classes. I was glad to get out of the cold and into the house. I checked the voicemail messages because Ted was unable to understand them. That day I had only one message from a college acquaintance, a legal colleague of Henry's, asking me to call her. When I called her, she told me that Henry had committed suicide. On an early morning hour before dawn, he went to his basement while his children and wife slept upstairs, and he shot himself in the temple. As she talked, I imagined the odor of seared flesh mingling with the smoke of the gun. She continued: "Henry left a note saying, 'I am tired of pretending to be someone I am not.'" During recent years, she said, he had been disbarred for taking a retainer from a client, then failing to follow through with the legal work.

After we hung up, I stared out at the leafless trees, naked in the cold of winter. My chest constricted, and I felt tears forming in my eyes for Henry, for a life he felt was useless.

I don't want to end up this way, in despair about my life choices..

If my marriage to Ted should end, I'll never marry again.

Foregone Conclusion
27

EARLY IN 1993, I decide to investigate treatment for Ted's alcoholism. I counsel with a psychologist, a recovering alcoholic herself. Dr. Elizabeth wants me to keep trying with Ted. Because she understands what it's like to be addicted, she doesn't want me to leave him. She wants me to work with him to deal with his addiction.

Maybe I can have a family intervention.

I gather literature on AA and give pamphlets to Ted. He refuses to look at them, throws them down on the dining room table.

Next, I try his son, Brad.

"Please, can you persuade your dad to attend a meeting?"

"I don't think Dad will go."

On Martin Luther King Day, a day off from teaching, I make an appointment with a doctor from a recovery program. It's in a Detroit hospital, downtown by the river. The program is for people like Ted, who are both addicted and disabled.

The office in which I wait is colorless, institutional. The chairs and tables are metal, the walls painted white. There is no one at the reception desk. I'm the only person in the room. I can feel the outside cold creeping into this old building.

I feel guilty, like a lover waiting for a tryst. I'm dishonest with my husband. I sneak around to find out about treatment for him while he resists every mention of help.

When the doctor finally comes into the room, he reminds me a bit of a physician in a horror movie asylum or Frankenstein's lab. He's the essence of white—his coat, his face, the skin on his folded hands as he listens to me.

He explains the treatment program, and how I will need to get Ted's cooperation to admit him into the hospital.

I drive home under Michigan's grey winter sky, dirty snow and slush melting under the tires of my car.

Will Ted ever consider this program? Fat chance.

At home, I show Ted the admission form and write him a note. "People with damage to the brain need a special kind of help with addictions."

He throws the paperwork on the table and walks out.

I sit alone at the dining room table where we've held so many of our discussions.

All that's left is a family intervention. I doubt that his family will participate. How can I ask them, or at least one of Ted's children, his daughter? I'm the culprit. I can imagine this response: "He's drinking because you ruined his marriage and his family." I have no energy to pursue it. I'm stuck, and I'm alone.

Two months pass. On a Friday night in late March, Ted and I attend a union dinner dance. All day long, the skies have been grey and have dealt us an early spring. I'm looking forward to an evening of music, dancing and good food, to break the winter spell. I'm wearing an off-the-shoulder, deep blue cocktail dress for the occasion.

I want to feel special. I want to have fun.

These union gatherings are important to Ted because he gave so much of his working life to the union. For years, he was on the negotiating team for faculty contracts. He was one of the early members of the chapter, coming to the college in 1957 after teaching at a local high school. Every time we attend a union event, Ted is surrounded by old friends, buddies from the earlier days of strikes, current officers of the union.

Tonight, he's dressed up in a rust-colored sport coat and the tie with a print of the Van Gogh's *Irises*. Ted loves Van Gogh's work, and I gave him the tie for his last birthday just days ago, on March 12. The blues of the painting soften the orange-rust flowers in the background, which matches his sport coat.

Van Gogh did the painting in 1890, one year before his death in the asylum in Saint Paul-de-Mausole, Provence, France. My mind pushes aside what I know of the occasion of the painting. It's a lush, gorgeous piece of work.

I'm elated to be at the dance, partly because I've detached myself from Ted. He's edgy and uncomfortable. After we choose a table, we head for the cash bar. With a glass of white wine, I mingle with friends and talk to a another teacher, Thomas, who likes to dance. I promise him a dance later. It's too noisy and too difficult for Ted to talk, so he sits at our table and drinks wine, one glass after another, as if he's in a drinking contest.

By the time the wait staff serves our plates of chicken cordon-bleu, Ted is drunk. He has not moved from his chair, but he's gone through several bottles of wine. He sways in his seat.

After dinner, the dancing starts. The college band plays "In the Mood," and I dance with Thomas. He twirls me around in a jitterbug until the room is lively. While we are dancing, I see Ted stagger across the room and disappear, I assume, into the men's bathroom. In between dances, Ted's good friend Ed stops by to ask me about him.

"I've just talked to Darlene and she commented that he doesn't look too good tonight."

I secretly agree with Ted's ex-wife, but I don't admit it. I don't want her to think I'm not making him happy.

Ten, fifteen minutes pass, and then twenty, twenty-five. Finally, I ask Ed, "Please check on Ted. He's been in the men's room for a long time."

He returns in only a minute.

"He's in bad shape. He's ill. You'd better take him home."

My stomach turns at the idea of a public scene. But I'm also relieved, as if a long-festering boil has finally been punctured.

With my coat over my arm, I walk to the men's room, where several of our colleagues stand around outside the open bathroom door. A man from the wait staff is trying to mop a generous mess from the floor.

Suddenly, it seems that the lobby of the hall is filled with people watching us, as someone helps me into my winter coat. I retrieve our car from the snowy parking lot and come back inside. The crowd near the restroom is still there, talking among themselves. In a surreal moment, I hear "Moonlight Serenade" as we walk out the automatic doors into the wet darkness.

During the drive home through the snow, Ted does not speak but stares out the window. When I turn corners, he sways back and forth in his seat. I drive cautiously because of the snow and ice. Icy rain hits the windshield, and I turn on the defroster to see the road.

I stop the car in the driveway near the side door so that I can help Ted get into the house. Before I have time to ring the bell, Owen opens the door and reaches out to help Ted. It's as if he's expecting us.

"Ted is extremely drunk. Please help me get him in the house."

I raise my voice. "And Owen, this is the last time you will ever have to see this."

As I reach for Ted's other arm to guide him into the house, he jerks it free. He shuffles downstairs to the basement, bumping his head on a low point in the ceiling, and goes straight to the shower.

That night I again sleep upstairs in the guest bed in the second floor. I curl tightly into a fetal position under blankets, all night long.

When I awake the next morning, I take the phone to the basement. I'll need privacy for this call to my friend Janice.

"I'm leaving Ted. I needed to say it out loud to someone."

As I hang up, Ted comes downstairs.

I say nothing, but my thoughts were clear.

Go away. I don't want you.

"Hold me, Nan."

I turn my face away from the stench of smoke in his skin and the sour wine on his breath.

I don't want you anymore. After all, of the months and years of hoping that you would admit that you have a problem. Now, you've proven it to everyone, to me, to your friends, to the whole world—and most of all to yourself.

A minute, two minutes, pass without a sound, other than his breathing against my chest. I push him away gently and walk upstairs to the dining room. At the table, I wait with pen and paper.

When he follows me and sits down, I write, "I'm done. I will not stay in this marriage. You're an alcoholic."

"Is there nothing left for me, Nan?" His voice pleads.

"Get professional help or we're finished."

"I'll do it myself; I don't need that bullshit." His voice turns to anger, a familiar, rough stubbornness.

I'm relieved.

ON EASTER SUNDAY a few weeks later, I sit at our kitchen table drinking coffee, trying to warm myself against another cold, wet spring day. Ted's oldest son, Adam, drops by the house to move some of his father's things into his truck. I hug him and offer him a cup of coffee.

"Nancy, I want you to know that we understand. We know you tried. We don't blame you for this divorce."

"Thanks. That means a great deal to me."

After Adam leaves, I pour myself another cup of coffee and sort through photos. I remember the good things about this marriage.

I think of Ted bringing home the red bike for Owen's eighth birthday, his struggle to make himself understood to the clerk at Sears as he handed him a pencil and paper.

Here is a picture with Ted and Owen, on Owen's ninth birthday. Owen's blond hair falls over his forehead. He smiles down at the two thick stacks of one-dollar bills, $500 total. Ted sits next to him, leaning slightly in his direction.

I remember Ted's generosity to me. He was always coming home with small gifts—exercise clothing, lingerie—and then a long string of large pearls.

What could I have done differently? Not loved him in the first place? Not married him after he had the stroke? Not confronted him about his habits?

I have no answers to these questions. I only know what I did and how it ended. I must embrace my life and accept what is now.

Holding On
28

TED TAKES A LONG TIME to move out. We put the house up for sale quickly after that evening, but there's no activity for weeks. Ted blames it on the signs I put in the yard supporting a millage for our school system. With our realtor Royce present, Ted yanks the signs from the lawn, leaving half-pulled clumps of grass. He shouts at us.

"You can't put out these signs when you're trying to sell the house!"

Royce and I remain calm. We wait for Ted to leave and then put the signs back on the front lawn.

Ted wants to give our Kenmore refrigerator to his son and his wife. Adam will pick up the fridge as soon as the house sells. Until then, Owen and I may use it for our food.

After a few weeks with no offers on the house, Ted becomes impatient. Every time he comes to collect boxes, he gestures to the refrigerator.

"Adam is waiting for this."

"I'll give him the refrigerator as soon as we move out. I'll scrub it until it's like new." I try to control the irritation in my voice.

My words didn't make any difference. Like an obsession, Ted still mentions the refrigerator every time he comes to the house.

It seems that small things provide the only way for him to express his anger and rejection.

Ted still has his house key, so every day he moves a few boxes to his car or his son's truck. One afternoon I return from teaching. I open the front door and sense he's been there. I look around—in the basement, in Owen's room upstairs, in our bedroom. The house is strangely barren-looking, even though I still have the furniture that belonged to me when we married. Then I realize that two stuffed toys are missing, a grey dog a friend made for Owen when he was born, and a bear with a t-shirt that reads "Gibson School," the private school he's attended since kindergarten. I paid $60 for that bear at a school auction so Owen could have a memento of his time there. He has one year left before he graduates from middle school.

Why would Ted keep Owen's stuffed animals? Did he take them to have something of Owen's, or is this a game?

I leave Ted a note on the kitchen table, where he will see it the next time he comes over.

"Ted, you accidentally packed Owen's stuffed dog and the bear from Gibson. Could you bring them back? They mean a lot to him and to me also. I paid $60 for the bear at an auction. Thanks!"

The next day, the dog and bear sit on our bare king-size mattress in the bedroom.

IN LATE APRIL, I run the three-mile Race-for-the-Cure at the Detroit Zoo. This is my third year to run this race. I don't run fast, but I'm steady. Since we moved into this brick bungalow in 1988, I've awakened at 5:30 a.m. at least three days a week to jog in the neighborhood. I wear radio headphones to help me get through the thirty-minute run. Week after week, I build up my strength for the spring race.

On this Saturday in late April, we have an icy rain, almost like snow. For some reason, the day seems to hold special possibility. I'm not sure why. I jog alongside a woman named Pam, a breast cancer survivor. On my t-shirt, I've pinned a sign— "I'm running for Pam." Pam was my best friend from high school who died of breast cancer at age 38.

I'm running with another Pam, a survivor.
In my own way, I'm a survivor. My friend Mary Jane said it.

We run by the giraffes and elephants, and the stench of feces from the elephant yard hits us in the face. We run by cages of exotic birds, their colors of orange and turquoise, yellow, puncturing the grey backdrop of the late spring cold.

We round a curve and turn toward the end of the race. Tired and sweaty, I push my wet bangs out of my eyes. I think I see Ted in the cheering crowd standing at the crossing line! He stands there on this cold, wet spring day, his wool cap pulled down over the top of his head just above his eyes, in his jeans and jacket, smoking a cigarette.

He's like a ghost haunting me with times that were happy and beautiful, sad and ugly.

DURING THE SUMMER while I wait for the house to sell, Ted leaves notes and buttons in our mailbox. One is an Amnesty International button with people holding hands—"We Are the Hope." On June 14, my birthday and our anniversary, I find a "Give Me a Birthday Kiss."

In July, I appear in the courtroom in the Wayne County Building.
I swear this is my last divorce.

Ted is not there. My lawyer and I stand before the judge and I answer his question, "Is this marriage irreconcilable?"

I do not hesitate.

"Yes."

IN DECEMBER Owen and I settle into our new house on Oak Street, a late 1940s, post-war bungalow with another full second-floor bedroom. This time, *I* will use the upstairs bedroom.

Our block of houses has the same design, though each house is distinguished by additions and architectural changes. I imagine

181

soldiers returning from World War II to live on this block with their families. I imagine the post-war prosperity, a 1950s neighborhood, with kids on bikes and wives at home, chatting with one another over fences while husbands work in an office or on the line at one of the Big Three, probably Ford, since Dearborn is the home of Henry Ford. This is Detroit, after all, a place of post-war hope for the American Dream.

My criteria for a perfect house are a fireplace, an attic bedroom, and a basement to refinish as a room for Owen. He needs privacy and space, now that he's almost thirteen years old. Our new house has all of these, and an enclosed room on the back that was once a porch, and a wood floor in the dining room.

And now, even though Owen and I do not fit the description of a traditional family, we will make a life here. I want this time in our lives to be special and safe. I'm hopeful that now, in this new home, Owen and I will have roots. He will graduate from middle school next June and begin high school in August.

No more husbands for Nancy.

WE MOVE INTO THE HOUSE on Oak Street on a wintry Saturday. This first Christmas season, a blizzard rattles the windows, and I with my son and mother (who moved to Michigan in May) enjoy the fireplace in a living room graced by my piano, familiar family pictures, and a framed, crocheted piece by my grandmother, Mama Steve Nelson.

In the new house, I hear from Ted again. He leaves a note in our mailbox.

In his last note to me, dated January 9, he asks for some help on an insurance paper.

"Nan, help me with insurance? Thank you. Ted."

For just a moment, I hesitate. *The old habit is there. I want to help him with more than business matters. I want to be there for him. I want to fix things.*

I must be careful not to fall back into my old patterns.

I call him to come by with the papers.

When he arrives, I struggle to detach myself. As we sit next to each other in my new dining room, at the same table where we had our "war councils," I feel drawn to him. I must stop myself from reaching over to touch his hand. I explain the insurance papers to him and show him where to sign. I see him watching me, perhaps hoping for a change, that I will come back.

I must free myself from my compulsion to save Dad.

And to save Ted.

Finding Dad
29

THAT LAST SUMMER of our marriage, when I packed up to move to a new house, I came across my miniature cedar chest, a gift from a Hartselle, Alabama, merchant to each of the high school seniors. When I opened the lid, the tangy cedar fragrance wafted upward, filling my head with the pungent memory of those warm May days when everything, the whole world, was ahead of me. Among the red, green, and yellow beads that my son Owen strung for me, the wooden flowers he painted blue in the third grade, was a small scrap of paper, a piece of a torn envelope. The words scrawled in fading pencil read: *Nancy, I am still alive and kicking a little bit. Love, Dad.*

IN AUGUST, a month after my divorce from Ted, I take a vacation alone to the Upper Peninsula. I leave on a Friday. My son is with his father in Alabama, so I'm free to set my pace for the trip the way I want, without considering anyone else's needs. I'm exhausted from my decision to leave Ted, from my struggle with another failed marriage.

I plan to take a day and a night on Mackinac Island. The next day, I will drive to Sault Ste. Marie, at the very top of the Upper Peninsula.

I board the ferry across to the island from St. Ignace, leaving my car in a parking lot. My seventh-grade class visited Mackinaw for our field trip in May of 1958. May is still close to winter in the Upper Peninsula. Mom chaperoned, and we all bundled together, our jackets pulled tight around our bodies, when we rode the ferry over. Those of us brave enough went swimming in the outside pool at the Grand Hotel. We came out in just a few minutes, shivering from the forty-degree water. The Grand Hotel was later the site of the film *Somewhere in Time* with characters who time travel to the late nineteenth century.

Like the characters in the film, today I am transported back in time as I walk about the island, buy fudge and take a carriage ride on the eight-mile drive around the island's edge. No cars are allowed here, and the streets are littered with horse manure. I could just as well be riding a carriage in the nineteenth century.

After dinner, I read a book in my second-floor hotel room overlooking the street. I hear people laughing and talking, the clopping of horses' hooves as they pass underneath my window.

The next morning, a Saturday, I buy fudge at one of the island fudge shops. I've waited to the end of my island visit so that I can hold onto the taste and texture of sweetness after I leave. I board the ferry back to the mainland.

The Mackinaw Bridge joins the two peninsulas, a span of almost five miles. It opened to traffic in November 1957. The bridge was still under construction when we moved to the Soo. I remember that long ferry ride home. Of course Taffy was with us, looking out the back window left and right, her tail twitching as she took in the strange new sights. It was a fall day, and the weather had started to turn cool. The sky was overcast.

As I cross the massive bridge, this clear August sky holds only a few cumulus clouds.

I drive the twenty-mile-an-hour speed limit, and I glance at water beneath me as I move across.

I'm headed for Sault Ste. Marie. I want to revisit the place of Dad's final Army assignment. The end of his career.

This is where he felt important as a military man.

BEFORE LEAVING DEARBORN, I had made a reservation in the Ojibway Hotel in downtown Soo. As an adolescent, I often passed by this very spot, walking with my friends to the locks to watch the freighters go through. I plan to spend two nights here and then head south on Monday morning toward home.

The most distinctive features of Sault Ste. Marie are the International Locks. I remember my time at twelve years old, watching the freighters being lowered by the locks from Lake Superior to the other Great Lakes because of a twenty-one-foot drop from Superior to the other bodies of water.

But today, I'm a grown woman, and the hotel has been renovated. Things have changed.

I check in, then enjoy a filet mignon, medium-well, baked potato, green salad, and a glass of Cabernet. I order chocolate cheesecake and coffee for dessert and take my time relishing the sweetness, as I read a few pages from a novel. I glance up every few minutes to look out of the restaurant windows at the boats gliding through the locks. I let my thoughts wander back to the time when I walked down to the locks with my friends to watch the boats pass through, just as they are passing through today.

I go to bed early so I'm fresh in the morning when I will explore places new and old.

ON SUNDAY MORNING I eat breakfast early and drive over the international bridge that connects the two Sault Ste. Maries—the Michigan and the Ontario cities. I find my way to the train station for a ride to Agawa Canyon, into the Canadian wilderness.

After a two-and-a-half-hour train ride through wilderness, our train arrives at the canyon. We tourists exit the train to stretch and look around this isolated provincial park. The attendant tells us that the only ways to travel here are by train, helicopter, or boat. We don't stay long. This is raw wilderness, no easy place to climb or hike. The point is the journey.

I record my impressions for later.

> *The train pulls up an incline,*
> *over a trestle—the valley falls away*
> *steep and deep in richness of greens,*
> *into fathomless lake-lands.*
>
> *At Agawa, paths encircle falling waters,*
> *sounds echo centuries ago. Here*
> *native people climbed rock faces*
> *and prayed*
> *to the sun.*

The return train ride is as beautiful as the first, with the sun moving toward the west to reveal subtle changes in the valley's shades of green. After we arrive back in Soo, Ontario, I'm so preoccupied with my impressions of the canyon that I drive through the international gate without stopping. The Canadian attendant chases me on foot, shouting "Hey, hey. STOP!" Embarrassed, I plead with him not to arrest me. I give him my business card and show him my college ID. Finally, he lets me go with a warning.

I'm lucky. In our post-9/11 world, I might have been shot, or sent to jail.

I'm distracted. I'm thinking about Dad.

BY LATE AFTERNOON, I'm back downtown, and I walk again down Portage Street by the locks. The seagulls squawk, float above the historical monument that commemorates the November 10, 1975 sinking of the *Edmund Fitzgerald* during the severe storm in the Great Lakes. The *Fitzgerald* passed through these very locks on its doomed voyage.

I hear the strains of Gordon Lightfoot's ballad about this deep and solemn Lake Superior, about the early storms in November that take men's bodies, never to be seen again.

After I pause to remember the men who died, I continue what now feels like a pilgrimage. I have a sense that no time has passed—not the thirty-three years of seconds, minutes, hours, days, or months since we drove out of Sault Ste. Marie, our car radio playing a "Canadian Sunset," my mother choking back tears.

I'm restless, so I drive around the town. I know that I'm searching for Dad in the lots of decayed foundations along Portage Street. I search for him near the Carnegie Library, now a school office, where he and I went to check out his Zane Grey novels and my romances and Dr. Doolittle books. I drive past our old house with two apartments. It's still green, but the paint is flaking off. I recall that we lived in both apartments, up, and then downstairs. Dad and I pitched balls in the front yard. I remember my friends coming to parties there, and I remember the time our cat Taffy disappeared, and then returned several days later to our front porch. She looked ragged, as if she had run for miles to get home to us. A resilient Taffy, she survived our moves from Texas to Missouri, then to Michigan. She always found her way home.

At last, I locate the National Guard Armory. I recall that the old one was torn down and this newer one built in the last months of our assignment here. I park my car in front and enter the heavy double doors. Inside, I see the bulletin board that looks familiar, covered with notices of guard activities and news, smell oil as my shoes squeak on the over-waxed floors. Guttural laughter and talk echo across the empty drill floor.

A soldier in camouflage approaches me.

"I'm here to see if you have any records of my father, Woodford Owen Nelson. Are there any documents?" I ask.

He leads me into the interior room where the men, just finished with Sunday drill, tilt their long-necked beers and talk in familiar comfort.

188

I ask my question again.

"My dad, Sergeant Nelson, was this unit's Army representative from 1958-1960."

A different soldier speaks.

"I remember Sarge Nelson! He took pride in his uniform. He was good to us, a good leader."

We look into the glass case for company photos of men from that period. The 1958-1960 pictures are not there.

If they're not in the company photos, where are they?

But I'm not disappointed. The soldier who spoke gives me the phone numbers of several retired men who knew Dad.

Back at my hotel room, I dial one of the numbers. The phone rings eight or ten times, and I'm about to hang up when a man finally answers.

"Hello?" His voice hesitates. He sounds old. I hope he recalls Dad. It's been a long time.

"I am Owen Nelson's daughter, Nancy. Sergeant Nelson. Do you remember him?"

His voice hesitates, and then he chuckles.

"Sure, I remember Sarge Nelson. He was so happy when I dropped off a case of Budweiser beer for him in Alabama. But seriously, he treated all the men with dignity. I'll never forget his pride when he came in his Lieutenant Colonel's uniform to the retirement party we gave him. He was a fine man, a fine man indeed."

As I listen to this man reminisce about Dad, I've just traveled back thirty years. I grip the phone tightly in my right hand. I struggle not to weep. I thank the soldier and hang up, stare at the walls of my hotel room. I barely hear the sounds of cars and raucous laughter from the bar across the street.

I speak aloud to a room that is no longer empty. "Dad, I can feel you here with me. Mom is well, and we both love you."

MONDAY MORNING, I begin the five-and-a-half-hour drive from Sault Ste. Marie to my Detroit suburb. As I drive south, I think about Dad and his flaws—his drinking, his inability to show

189

affection, his silence when I needed talk. After his death, my efforts to find him in other men—in their passivity, anger, or illness—were vain attempts to retrace my journey to reach him in my first twenty-three years of life, before his death.

I view my father now without fear or shame, his, or mine.

Owen Nelson battled depression and the pain of failure for his whole life. When he was young, he went into the world with the promise of being a holy man and instead became an ordinary soldier. He carried a deep faith and hope for the human race, and he hated cruelty and dishonesty. He watched his brother become a successful banker and his sisters marry men established in the community. Always, the specter of his parents' disappointment hung over him, a reminder of his failure.

He loved my mother passionately and deeply even though he struggled, especially in later years, to express this love beyond an expensive gift or a pinch or pat.

In many ways, he willed his early death. I saw him die long before he breathed his last. I read the anguish in his distraction and his silences late at night as he watched reruns of "The Untouchables" or "Gunsmoke". He couldn't abide to think about what he had seen, the secrets of his military life, his own failure.

Yet he was also full of fun and mischief. There was an indefatigable quality about him that drew people to him, a quality of humor and compassion and kindness. I was reminded of this again recently, as I leafed through his World War II scrapbook. On a note he left about an evening event he wrote:

Sat with the colonel and his wife at the dinner dance.
Did not have to dance and therefore had a good time.

I missed my father even when he was still alive. I should have known then what I know now—that he could not give me any more love than he did. That he gave love in ways I didn't recognize.

And I'll take them all, those examples of his love. I'll remember his fairness to people, his insistence that everyone, no matter what race or religion, deserves respect and a chance at the American dream. His refusal to turn blacks away from our church door and his anonymous gifts to poor children in my sister Betty's class. I'll remember his commitment to his work, to our country, his Bible study, the way he prepared lessons like a preacher, page after page of notes and outlines, in an effort to make his faith relevant, and even challenging and visionary, to adults in a small town in 1960s Alabama.

I can stop looking for Dad. He's been here all the time. He's here with me now, talking to me in ways I always wanted us to talk when he was alive. When I become passionate about issues in society or angry at inequity and cruelty, I can hear him speak to me.

"Nancy, I am still alive and kicking a little bit. Love, Dad."

Endings

30

MARCH 12, 1995. It's Ted's sixty-fifth birthday and the twenty-seventh anniversary of Dad's death. I've always thought it ironic that the date of Dad's death is Ted's birthday, as if the date represents a cycle of life and death.

However, on this Sunday morning, I don't think of Ted. We've been divorced for over a year.

Instead, I take a brisk walk with my friend Mary. It's chilly, still officially winter, but some early new grass peeks through the snow. We walk fast to bring up our pulse rates, and even in the cool morning, sweat forms on my chest and back.

Back home, I find a message on the answering machine.

"Nancy, this is Brad. Please call me."

Ted's son Brad has kept me informed about his dad since Ted and I divorced. Ted moved back into an apartment in the same city. Darlene offered him furniture, which he refused. The fall before this, Ted had abdominal surgery, and he recovered and went home to his apartment in Inkster. I sent a card to the hospital. I was too late. The card was returned unopened, with "Return to Sender" stamped on the back of the envelope.

Today, Brad's voice on the message sounds no different than usual. In a hurry to leave for my book group, I write myself a reminder to call later.

Back home at 6:00, I call Brad.

His wife Janice answers. "Nancy, Ted has committed suicide."

I feel sick, as if I'll faint or throw up.

"We'll be right over." I hang up quickly.

"Owen, come upstairs now. Something bad has happened." My voice trembles.

Owen comes right away. He might have ignored me with his fourteen-year-old nonchalance, but today he knows my voice sounds urgent.

"Ted has killed himself."

"We're going to Brad and Janice's house."

Now my voice is a choked whisper.

Owen says nothing, just puts on his sneakers and grabs his jacket.

Brad and Janice live only a few blocks away.

When we arrive, Brad and Adam are coming back from the funeral home. Brad speaks first.

"Apparently, Dad planned this carefully. On Friday night, he prepared his business papers and laid out instructions for his monies and insurance on a coffee table in the living room of his apartment. He left a Petoskey stone, polished and shining, with a piece of paper that said, 'For E.,' my aunt who especially likes his polished stones. Then he called me to make an appointment for yesterday morning. I arrived about eleven. I thought it was to help Dad with some business papers. I found him."

As I imagine it, Ted cut his wrists and bled until sometime in the early morning hours, he stopped breathing, one day before his sixty-fifth birthday.

As I listen to Brad talk, I envision Ted as he lies in the bathtub. I do not ask, but I think he would choose that place to contain his blood so that it can be easily cleaned up.

Adam says the EMS guys weren't too kind when they arrived for the body.

"*Rigor mortis* had set in. They had a hard time moving him into the ambulance, so they made jokes about it."

As I sit next to Owen on Brad's and Janice's couch, I realize my first response to this news: I'm not surprised. *I understand why Ted committed suicide. He was a man who loved life and women and language and beauty, and he could no longer tolerate living with his limitations, his addictions. In his heart he would always be a writing teacher and a poet. He was rendered powerless by a blood clot that destroyed the brain cells he had used to make poems, to teach, to make love.*

I also understand why Ted had Brad find him. Yes, it seems brutal to leave your son the life-long memory of finding your stiffened body. But Brad is the closest, the most like Ted. He's built like his dad, plays basketball, and has the same passion for life. Brad is the one who supported his dad through the divorce from his mother. He's always kind to me when he could have blamed me for destroying his parents' marriage.

In a strange way, Ted gave Brad a gift, a final ritual that represents their special connection. Like a tribal rite.

I know how Ted would think. *Have my son, the person closest to me, find and take care of my body. He'll understand.*

AT THE FUNERAL, Owen and I stand together next to Ted's casket. He's dressed in his "wedding and funeral suit" and wears the Van Gogh Irises tie I gave him, the one he wore to the fated dinner dance. Ted's quip about his suit is not funny today.

Owen and I weep.

For the service, my son and I sit three rows behind Ted's other family. Owen wears a World Cup Soccer tie Ted sent him for his last birthday. We are flanked by friends who have come to support us. I think they understand the awkwardness we feel even in the midst of our grief.

Ted's friends and colleagues share thoughts, stories and memories about Ted. Our union president gives the major address. He celebrates Ted's life, recalling his years of service to the College and the union, his generosity to friends, his loving pride in his children, his "unflinching integrity, energy, compassion, and courage." The president has known Ted many years before I was hired. He knows of his steadfastness and fairness in union negotiations

He then reads "The Poet," by Thomas Hardy. Hardy writes of a man who did not care "For loud acclaim," a man loved by two women:

> *Come to his graveside, pause and say:*
> *"Whatever his message—glad or grim—*
> *Two bright-souled women clave to him";*
> *Stand and say that, while day decays;*
> *It will be word enough of praise... .*

"*Two bright-souled women.*" Darlene and me. And neither of us could save him.

I tried, and I'm sure she did too.

Finally, he calls on both of Ted's families, thanking each of us by name for "sacrifices you made which enabled him to teach, befriend, and support us."

My throat tightens.

What have I done to help him?

I stayed with Ted when he became ill, his brain ravaged by a stroke. Some will say I took him from his rightful family. But did I really? He wanted me. He made that choice before the stroke. Perhaps what I did give him, for as long as I could, was the dignity of his choices.

I left only when I could no longer stay in the battle.

What about Dad? It's as if I had another chance with Ted to try to help my father. It's as if I needed the chance to see that, like Ted's, all of Dad's flaws were his own, as mine are my own. That the life of transience and addiction does not have to destroy me.

It's as if I'm ready now to own my life.

My choices must be mine, and mine alone. I give responsibility to no one else.

AFTER THE FUNERAL SERVICE, Ted's family, colleagues, and friends, mingle for last words. A friend pulls me aside. "You took care of him, Nancy. You loved him when others struggled to."

As Owen and I move toward the exit, another friend, Sue, grasps my elbow and turns me around. She heads across the room toward Darlene.

"You need to speak to her, Nancy."

My steps toward Darlene take a long time. We've seen one another only at school, where we can be distant. When I come face to face with her tonight in the room where the body of the man we both loved lies, we look straight into one another's eyes.

I speak first. "I am very sorry."

"I am sorry too for your loss." Her voice is strong.

I believe she knows my grief. I believe she gives me the right to mourn.

Beginnings
31

2015

Dear Dad,

I want to talk to you about my life.

I'm not the same person you knew, or thought you knew, when you died in 1968. I haven't had the best personal record. I'm in my fifth marriage. I've been with many men, and I've made mistakes. You would shudder if you knew the details of my personal life. You would be happy, though, to know that some good things came out of it all.

You have another grandson, Owen, named after you. One time when he was angry with his own father, he thought about changing his last name to Nelson. I said I'd be proud to have another Owen Nelson in my life. But as an adult, Owen has reunited with his father Bill, who has become a different person due to his own painful experiences. Bill and Owen are talking.

I've told Owen about you—all of it. He knows about your troubles with drinking, your depression and despair. He knows, too, how you helped other people, and how you taught your daughters not to hate. As I look back on my marriage to his father, I understand more clearly why Bill and I did not stay together. We were both wounded, Bill by an angry, troubled father, and I by you, a man who saw injustice in the world, hated it, and drank to soothe his pain. I know that, sometimes, my anger may have provoked Bill's. "It takes two to tango," as they say.

Bill and I are several years apart in age. I was close to earning my PhD when I met him. He had yet to finish his BA. It must have been hard on him to take classes from professors whom I had known academically. While we fit into each other's friend groups, there was often a sense of being out of rhythm with one another, maybe like you and Mom, when you were off with your military friends and she was raising her girls and fulfilling the "military wife" role.

Bill and I are both Geminis, with birthdays one day apart. Some sources say that Geminis can marry or cohabit well, but it takes luck and effort. Obviously, it didn't work for us.

You would be happy to know that Mom had many good years of life after you left. She lived to be ninety-six, and in her last years, she moved to Michigan to be near me, Owen, and my husband Roger. We watched over her. She never stopped talking to you and thinking about you.

My husband Roger is my best friend. I know you'd like him, probably love him. For part of his life, he grew up on a farm. He knows the meaning of hard work. He spent years as an engineer, in one place, like you spent years in your one job, but in many places.

Roger has been good to Owen. He became a dad to him when Owen's biological father Bill was unable to be there for him. Roger was also good to Mom. He visited her, and they listened to poetry and music. He took her for walks in her wheelchair, and he painted her fingernails. He was with her, and me, when she died.

Owen's father and I have reconciled as friends. For the decades when we were alienated, Bill's sister never stopped being my friend. She loved everyone and wanted everyone to love one other. Instead of calling me her "ex-sister-in-law," which she thought was a cold label, she called me her "sister-in-love" and never stopped treating me as part of the family, even though she had to be discreet. With her recent passing, I have felt a real closeness to Bill, one that transcends differences and years. I see Mary as the light of peace and hope between us. One of her wishes before her death was that her brother, her nephew, and her sister-in-love would find connection again. Sometimes the power of love does prevail. Her wish was answered.

Here's the best:

Ten years ago, Owen and his wife had a beautiful baby girl, Laura Camila. Your great-granddaughter. Mi nieta. *Our bloodline. She grows tall and beautiful.*

I love you, Dad,
Nancy

POSTLUDE:
A Healing

I HAVE EVERYTHING I need for my life to make sense. But something is missing. I'm plagued by dreams of my father, his sadness, dreams of Ted, his anger and dissolution.

On a May morning, I visit my friend Jane, a healer. We talk quietly for a few minutes, sitting on the floor of her ceremony room. I tell her about my father, about my fourth husband, how he cut his wrists and bled to death almost two years after our divorce.

Jane tells me she will sing my father and my husband to the light.

"A sweet death song," she says.

She covers me with a thin sheet. I've taken off my shoes and socks; and her cat, Ash, sits on my chest, kneading me and nibbling on my blouse buttons. I close my eyes and Jane shakes a rattle toward each direction, sings songs of blessing and peace.

After the four directions, Jane sings, "Go to the light." I let my body sink deeper onto the table, let my feet fall out to the sides, and my arms lie loose beside my body. Every minute or so, I stroke Ash, and he nibbles on my fingers. He leaves, and then returns.

I imagine a lighted gate, an opening that draws troubled spirits toward rest.

In an instant, Jane's voice stops. My feet, my body, are suddenly cold, as if someone has opened a window.

"How do you feel?" the healer asks in a whisper.

"I'm cold. The room became cold when you stopped singing."

"That's when they left, your dad and your husband. I recognized them both. Ted looked around to see where he was, then took off really fast. He was glad to leave. Your dad was heavy and sad. It was like removing a boulder from the side of a mountain. But when he left, he was full of love."

Steaming Concrete

1986

In spring, I am a rose's thorn.
I leave safety, colorful
streets with florid gardens,
leave for speechless love,
damaged brain, aphasia.

This dark summer bears no fruit,
no roses where he and my son
dribble basketballs again and again.
Their bunce, a hollow heavy heart,
pounds on steaming concrete.

In eight years, he will cut his wrists,
drain his body overnight.
Rigor mortis in the morning.

But today
he brings me a rose.
Though cut too soon,
its petals are soft, fragrant.
Only one frees itself,
falls,
as he places the flower
in my hand.

Nancy Owen Nelson

ABOUT THE AUTHOR

RAISED IN HARTSELLE, ALABAMA, Nancy Owen Nelson has published articles in several academic journals and anthologies and has co-edited and edited academic books. Her poetry is published in *What Wildness is This?* (University of Texas Press, March 2007), *South Dakota Review* and *Graffiti Rag,* and her creative nonfiction pieces in *Mom's Writing Literary Journal* (Fall, 2008), *Lalitamba Journal,* and *Roll* (Telling Our Stories Press, 2013). Her memoir, *Searching for Nannie B: Connecting Three Generations of Southern Women,* was published by Ardent Writer Press in 2015, and her poetry books, *My Heart Wears No Colors* (FutureCycle Press), 2018, and *Portals: A Memoir in Verse* (Kelsay Books) in 2019.

CPSIA information can be obtained
at www.ICGtesting.com
Printed in the USA
LVHW050441230621
690929LV00013B/1898